Best Climbs
Santa Barbara
and Ventura

DAMON CORSO

GUILFORD, CONNECTICUT
HELENA, MONTANA

FALCONGUIDES®

An imprint of Rowman & Littlefield
Falcon, FalconGuides, and Chockstone are registered trademarks and Make Adventure Your Story is a trademark of Rowman & Littlefield.

Distributed by NATIONAL BOOK NETWORK

British Library Cataloguing-in-Publication Information available

Library of Congress Cataloging-in-Publication Data
Names: Corso, Damon.
Title: Best climbs Santa Barbara and Ventura / Damon Corso.
Description: Guilford, Connecticut : FalconGuides, [2016] | "Distributed by
    NATIONAL BOOK NETWORK"—T.p. verso. | Includes index.
Identifiers: LCCN 2016018507 (print) | LCCN 2016025333 (ebook) | ISBN
    9781493016549 (paperback : alk. paper) | ISBN 9781493026975 (e-book)
Subjects: LCSH: Mountaineering—California—Guidebooks. |
    Trails—California—Guidebooks. | California—Guidebooks.
Classification: LCC GV199.42.C2 C67 2016 (print) | LCC GV199.42.C2 (ebook) |
    DDC 796.52209794—dc23
LC record available at https://lccn.loc.gov/2016018507

∞™ The paper used in this publication meets the minimum requirements of American National Standard for Information Sciences—Permanence of Paper for Printed Library Materials, ANSI/NISO Z39.48-1992.

WARNING

Climbing is a sport where you may be seriously injured or die. Read this before you use this book.

This guidebook is a compilation of unverified information gathered from many different climbers. The author cannot ensure the accuracy of any of the information in this book, including the topos and route descriptions, the difficulty ratings, and the protection ratings. These may be incorrect or misleading, as ratings of climbing difficulty and danger are always subjective and depend on the physical characteristics (for example, height), experience, technical ability, confidence, and physical fitness of the climber who supplied the rating. Additionally, climbers who achieve first ascents sometimes underrate the difficulty or danger of the climbing route. Therefore, be warned that you must exercise your own judgment on where a climbing route goes, its difficulty, and your ability to safely protect yourself from the risks of rock climbing. Examples of some of these risks are falling due to technical difficulty or due to natural hazards such as holds breaking, falling rock, climbing equipment dropped by other climbers, hazards of weather and lightning, your own equipment failure, and failure or absence of fixed protection.

You should not depend on any information gleaned from this book for your personal safety; your safety depends on your own good judgment, based on experience and a realistic assessment of your climbing ability. If you have any doubt as to your ability to safely climb a route described in this book, do not attempt it.

The following are some ways to make your use of this book safer:

1. Consultation: You should consult with other climbers about the difficulty and danger of a particular climb prior to attempting it. Most local climbers are glad to give advice on routes in their area; we suggest that you contact locals to confirm ratings and safety of particular routes and to obtain firsthand information about a route chosen from this book.

2. Instruction: Los Angeles County has a strong community of local climbing instructors and guides available; a list is provided in the appendix. We recommend that you engage an instructor or guide to learn safety techniques and to become familiar with the routes and hazards of the areas described in this book. Even after you are proficient in climbing safely, occasional use of a guide is a safe way to raise your climbing standard and learn advanced techniques.

3. Fixed Protection: Some of the routes in this book may use bolts and pitons that are permanently placed in the rock. Because of variances in the manner of place-ment, weathering, metal fatigue, the quality of the metal used, and many other fac-tors, these fixed protection pieces should always be considered suspect and should always be backed up by equipment that you place yourself. Never depend on a single piece of fixed protection for your safety, because you never can tell whether it will hold weight. In some cases, fixed protection may have been removed or is now miss-ing. However, climbers should not always add new pieces of protection unless exist-ing protection is faulty. Existing protection can be tested by an experienced climber and its strength determined. Climbers are strongly encouraged not to add bolts and drilled pitons to a route. They need to climb the route in the style of the first ascent party (or better) or choose a route within their ability—a route to which they do not have to add additional fixed anchors.

Be aware of the following specific potential hazards that could arise in using this book:

1. Incorrect Descriptions of Routes: If you climb a route and you have a doubt as to where it goes, you should not continue unless you are sure that you can go that way safely. Route descriptions and topos in this book could be inaccurate or misleading.

2. Incorrect Difficulty Rating: A route might be more difficult than the rating indi-cates. Do not be lulled into a false sense of security by the difficulty rating.

3. Incorrect Protection Rating: If you climb a route and you are unable to arrange adequate protection from the risk of falling through the use of fixed pitons or bolts and by placing your own protection devices, do not assume that there is adequate protection available higher just because the route protection rating indicates the route does not have an X or an R rating. Every route is potentially an X (a fall may be deadly), due to the inherent hazards of climbing—including, for example, failure or absence of fixed protection, your own equipment's failure, or improper use of climb-ing equipment.

There are no warranties, whether expressed or implied, that this guidebook is accurate or that the information contained in it is reliable. There are no warranties of fitness for a particular purpose or that this guide is merchantable. Your use of this book indicates your assumption of the risk that it may contain errors and is an acknowledgment of your own sole responsibility for your climbing safety.

Contents

Santa Barbara and Ventura Overview

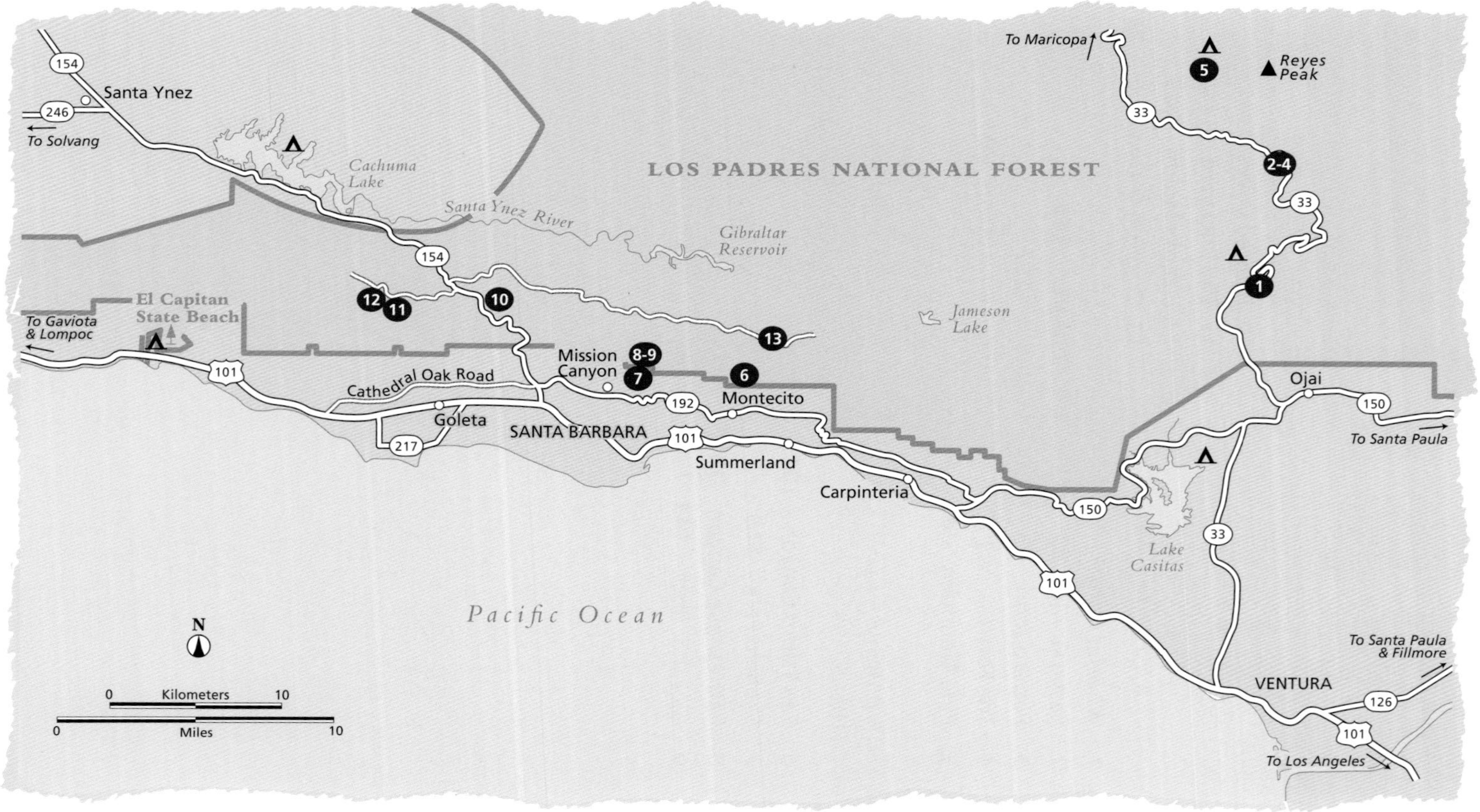

Acknowledgments

A climbing guide is a passion project, and it is impossible to attain the highest possible passion for something without an influx of past and present experiences from members across the community. Without the dedication of the major players in Santa Barbara and Ventura, this book wouldn't be possible. Rocks were "discovered," trails were cut, poison ivy was contracted, and projects were sent, and this pattern was followed decade after decade starting with the area's originator, Herbert Rickert. From Herb's first ascents at Gibraltar Rock and Sespe Gorge in the 1950s, to Yvon Chouinard attracting world-class athletes to the region in the 1960s, all the way to the latest high-end additions in the area from Bernd Zeugswetter, Andy Patterson, and Sean Crozier, Santa Barbara and Ventura may never "tap out" of good rock.

The following people have been instrumental in developing and nurturing climbing in Santa Barbara and Ventura, and have in some form or manner been a part of the creation of this guidebook and deserve a huge thank-you: Bob Banks, Andy Patterson, Mary Patterson, Bernd Zeugswetter, Hjördis Rickert, Matthew Fienup, Bryson Fienup, Sean Naugle, Steve Tucker, Kevin Steele, Herbert Rickert, Dave Armstrong, Rick Knight, John Hestenes, Yvon Chouinard, Bob McTavish, Sir Chris Bonnington, Dick Blankenbecler, William Thompson, Hans Florine, Jim Donini, Henry Barber, Wills Young, Reese Martin, Arvind Gupta, The Castle, Stuart Ruckman, Tony Agulara, Mike Gould, Liza Butler, Alex Bury, Reese Martin, Matt Polk, Dan Frame, Romain Wacziarg, Jesse Groves, Tim Nelson, Kip Gerenda, Garrett Gregor, Chris Lindner, Crystalyn Corso, Buck Branson, Cary Carmichael, Chris Broomell, Paul Dusatko, Natasha Barnes, Sean Crozier, Sean Denny, Joe Roland, Chuck Fitch, Steve Fitch, Kevin Brown, Rick Mosher, Jeff Smith, Curt Dixon, John Chavez, Mike Forkash, Pat Shourds, Jim Tobish, John Mireles, Marc Soltan, John Perlin, Todd Mei, Doug Hsu, Jason Houston, Viju Mathieu, Rick Freidland, Russell Erickson, Scott London, Stephen Duneier, Mike Colee, Thomas Townsend, Amos Clifford, Gary Anderson, Galen MacDougall, Elijah Ball, Becca Polglase, and Geneva Damico. Lastly we cannot forget the renaissance man of Santa Barbara, Steve Edwards; may he forever rest in peace. Thanks also to anyone else who has or plans on setting foot in one of these majestic climbing areas.

Herb Rickert making an early ascent
with hemp ropes and wooden pegs
on Gibraltar rock in the early 1950s
PHOTO DAVE ARMSTRONG

Introduction

Resting in the midst of California's version of the Riviera are thousands of boulders and dozens of cliffs just waiting for the sun to peek through the morning clouds and bring another great climbing day to the coast. Santa Barbara and Ventura are full of climbing history reaching all the way back to the early 1950s with the likes of Yvon Chouinard, record speed climber Hans Florine, originator Herb Rickert, and Jim Donini, Henry Barber, Steve Edwards, Bob Banks, Kevin Steele, and Wills Young gracing these sun-soaked rocks. Although the region has just recently been put on the map for its unmatched sandstone bouldering, its sport and traditional routes should not be forgotten. If you surf, you'll want to drop into "C-Street" in Ventura near the fairgrounds for its stellar point breaks, or just relax on one of the pristine Santa Barbara County state beaches like Refugio or El Capitan. Don't forget to check out one of the natural hot springs the region has to offer.

This book will give you all the information necessary to access the natural rock treasures that Ventura and Santa Barbara have to offer to outdoor climbing enthusiasts. The rock quality, purity of the lines, and beautiful surroundings will provide experiences you can enjoy and help preserve for generations to come.

How to Use This Guide

The sport routes, topropes, traditional climbs, and boulder problems in this book have been selected from the thousands of lines in Ventura and Santa Barbara Counties based on their rock quality; purity of line (natural lines of weakness up the cliff); fun, interesting, unique, or noteworthy climbing; existing climber's access trails; and approaches and descents that do not cause degradation to the fragile environment.

Directions (e.g., "go right" or "climb up and left," etc.) are given as if you are facing the route. Routes are generally listed from left to right as you face the cliff. Directions for climbing down, descending, rappelling, and so on are given for the same orientation (as if you were facing the route from the start of the route). Generally routes are descended by a standard rappel, and boulder problems have an obvious descent or walk off, unless otherwise noted.

On most routes, pitch lengths (e.g., 80 feet) are given; these are estimates and not exact figures. Route lines drawn on the photo topos are approximations; every effort has been made to depict the exact line of the route, but as always, trust your own judgment. Dangerous routes have been listed with an "R" rating, and caution is advised when attempting one of these routes.

Difficulty Ratings

The difficulty rating system used in this guidebook for roped routes is the Yosemite Decimal System (YDS), the system used throughout the United States. Climbing routes are rated on an ascending scale from 5.0 (the easiest climbs requiring ropes and belays) to 5.15 (currently the most difficult climbs). Within the 5.10, 5.11, 5.12, 5.13, 5.14, and 5.15 categories, the subgrades of a, b, c, and d are used to denote finer distinctions in difficulty.

The "V" rating scale, which is used for the boulder problems in this guidebook, has become the standard boulder grading scale in the United States. Boulder problems are rated on an ascending scale from V0 (the easiest problems) to V16 (currently the most difficult boulder problems).

A climb may feel harder for some and easier for others depending on one's height, arm span, leg span, and so on. Over time you should get a feel for the grading scale and be able to make your own decisions; the grades are offered only to give you a general sense of difficulty.

A PG13 rating reflects a route that is moderately risky with some unprotected moves, while an R rating reflects a route that is very risky and a fall can lead to serious injury.

Geology

Geologically, the Ventura and Santa Barbara area, which lies mainly within Los Padres National Forest, is complex and composed of the Transverse and Coastal Ranges. Along the coast, massive beach cliffs wither away with erosion from the waves. The Transverse Ranges run east to west along the San Andreas Fault where the tectonic shifts from the North American Plate and the Pacific Plate have pushed these mountains to heights ranging from 3,000 to 8,000 feet in elevation. Over the millennia, before the uprising of these

A lone surfer in the early morning hours
PHOTO MATTHEW FIENUP

mountain ranges, many layers of sediment and minerals were deposited across the area; these layers can be most noticeably seen along the Topatopa Mountains just north of Ojai. Within the Transverse Ranges lie hot springs and geological hazards such as earthquakes and landslides. Along with constant change in the current geology comes the discovery of both vertebrate and invertebrate fossils, millions of years old, scattered throughout the region.

The rock in this region varies from Matilija Sandstone and Coldwater Sandstone to cobbled conglomerate and metamorphic blueschist from the Franciscan Assemblage. Because most of the climbing in this book is on some form of sandstone, it is imperative that climbers wait at least three days after a rainstorm to test the rock. There have been wet seasons in Santa Barbara where the rock hasn't dried out until early July, but this is rare. The Matilija Sandstone can be seen most prominently at Gibraltar Rock, Sespe Gorge, and Wheeler Gorge; it is a somewhat harder variance of the sandstones in the area. The Coldwater Sandstone is eminent at San Ysidro Canyon and Skofield Park, and is a much softer variance that tends to be a lot easier on the skin. Due to this region's soft sandstone, many unique features exist; for example, ripples can be seen on the larger formation at Gibraltar. The ripples are known as conchoidal fracture planes, where a large chunk of rock has fallen off, exposing how water affected the outcome of these particular sedimentary layers. Chemical weathering is another effect you can see most dominantly in the main overhangs at Lizard's Mouth and the Brickyard; webs of pockets can be seen here where natural lime and salts have eaten away at the integrity of the rock.

Last, you will notice a fair amount of cracks in the Ventura and Santa Barbara region. These cracks were formed by tectonic shifting, plant life growing, and water freezing and expanding inside small fractures. Gold and precious minerals were a significant part of these regions and are mined to this day. Oil and gas are also being pumped from rocks deep below the surface at a handful of oil fields still in operation.

Preparation

To prepare for climbing outdoors on real rock, it is best to familiarize yourself with the sport of rock climbing by joining a rock climbing gym and taking one of their available courses or by taking a rock climbing class or guided trip with an outdoor climbing guiding service (see appendix). Be sure to have all permits needed for the area where you plan to climb (see "Wilderness Permit Requirements" below), and check the "Equipment and Essentials List" to ensure you have a safe and fun experience. Make sure you are familiar with the poison oak plant, because it can be found at most of the crags in this book. A good tip is to apply rubbing alcohol anywhere you may have come in contact with poison oak; the alcohol will break down the oils before they have time to penetrate your skin. Carry a small bottle of rubbing alcohol or hand sanitizer when on trips in this region.

Climbing Seasons

Climbing is possible year-round in Santa Barbara and Ventura Counties. The only time climbing is not possible is during and after a rainstorm; please allow at least three days for the rock to dry out. Sometimes it may take longer, and it helps when the winds pick up and the sun comes out multiple days in a row. The rock is very brittle and has been known to break. The most desirable seasons to climb are autumn, winter, and spring. Climbing is still possible in the heat of the summer, but you will be chasing shade and running from bugs most of the time. The best time to climb in the summer is at first light and from just before sunset until it's dark out. The Mediterranean climate of the coastline lends itself to great climbing weather—the average low-high temperature is 55–70°F, with an average of thirty-seven days of precipitation. Many mornings begin with a thick coastal fog that forms due to the hot temperatures from the Santa Ynez Valley colliding with the cool winds coming off the Pacific Ocean. Typically around noon the fog will burn off, leaving a perfect bluebird day.

Equipment and Essentials List
- Helmet
- Rope (60 meters/197 feet of 9.5 to 11mm diameter) for most areas. Certain areas as noted require a 70-meter (230-foot) rope or two 70-meter ropes for rappels; see each area for more information.
- Harness
- Carabiners (2 locking D)

An Anna's hummingbird and its chicks, a rare treat at San Ysidro Canyon
Photo Matthew Fienup

- Traditional climbing rack (full set of nuts/Stoppers, full set of cams 0.5 to 4 inches). Certain areas require a double rack for specific routes; see each route for details.
- 8 to 14 quickdraws (depending on the area)
- Webbing/slings/cordage
- Sunglasses
- Water/windproof shell
- First-aid kit
- Sunburn protection (sunblock/hat)
- Flashlight and/or headlamp
- Knife for cutting rope
- Water
- Snacks/food

Land Management and Closures

The area around the walking trail to San Ysidro Canyon is private property; the trail passes through the property of a boutique hotel and restaurant, so please be mindful of the amount of noise you make, and be sure to stay on the main walking trail into the canyon where the national forest begins. The climbing at the Painted Cave Boulders is also next to private residences; please respect the neighbors and be aware of the noise level and where you place your pads. At the Lizard's Mouth you are climbing just down the slope from the Winchester Canyon Gun Club (www.wcgc.com); please respect the boundaries and be aware of your safety if wandering out of the main climbing areas.

No-Trace Ethic

You can practice Leave No Trace principles from the moment you step out of your car. Always use the marked trails and climber's paths when available. If there is no marked trail to the cliff, minimize your impact by walking on durable surfaces (e.g., a rock slab or barren ground).

The perfect spot for a hot summer afternoon: a lazy river and hidden boulders strewn about

If nature calls and you are far away from any outhouse, deposit solid human waste well away from the base of any climbing site or water source by digging a cathole 8 inches deep. Cover and disguise the cathole when done. Pack out all toilet paper and tampons in a baggie. Urinate on base ground of rock, not plants. Urine contains salt, and animals will dig into plants to get to it.

Respect the resident wildlife. Pick up all food crumbs, and don't feed any animals—this habituates them to human food and encourages them to beg and scavenge for more food. Keep an eye on your pack at the base of any cliff; squirrels will chew right through it to get food.

For more information on outdoor climbing ethics, visit www.LNT.org or the Access Fund website at www.accessfund.org.

Wilderness Permit Requirements

Los Padres National Forest requires a National Forest Adventure Pass for day-use parking. You can purchase a day pass or an annual pass at any of the outdoor gear vendors in Ventura or Santa Barbara and at 7-11s, gas stations, or local markets near the national forest. They can also be found at the ranger station at the Ojai Ranger District, 1190 East Ojai Ave., Ojai, CA 93023, (805) 646-4348; the Santa Barbara Ranger District, 3505 Paradise Rd., Santa Barbara, CA 93105, (805) 967-3481; or online at www.kinsale.com or www.myscenicdrives.com.

To Report Climbing Accidents

In most areas, to report a climbing accident or other emergency, dial 911. Cell phones are the usual method of reporting accidents and summoning rescues, but they don't work everywhere in the mountains, especially if not fully charged before you get to the climbing destination, where cell service is sometimes questionable. If you cannot contact a 911 operator, dial "0" and ask for the emergency dispatch operator or county sheriff. The county sheriff is responsible for coordinating mountain rescue operations in most areas.

Moonrise over Los Padres National Forest

Climb Finder

Best Boulder Problems
- Lizard's Mouth Traverse, V0 and up, Lizard's Mouth
- Fifteen Years on Ice, V0, Pine Mountain
- Chunks O' Flesh, V1, Skofield Park
- Buckets Forever, V2, Rattlesnake Canyon
- Quiet Soul, V2, Pine Mountain
- Painted Carnival, V3, Pine Mountain
- Heaven on Top, V3, Pine Mountain
- Meilee, V3/4, Lizard's Mouth
- Yeti, V4, The Brickyard
- Mutants Amok, V5, Skofield Park

Best Single-Pitch Sport Routes
- The Ecstasy of Gold, 5.8, Crag Full O' Dynamite
- Cobble Climb, 5.8, Wheeler Gorge
- Permanent Income Hypothesis, 5.9, The Fortress
- The Good, the Bad, and the Ugly, 5.9, Crag Full O' Dynamite
- The Great Race, 5.10a, San Ysidro Canyon
- Sword in the Stone, 5.10a, Rattlesnake Canyon

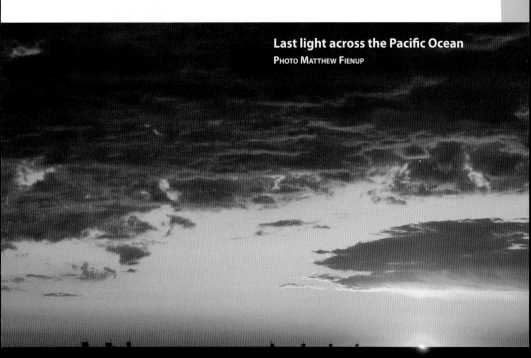

Last light across the Pacific Ocean
PHOTO MATTHEW FIENUP

Goulara, 5.10c/5.11+, Wheeler Gorge
A Route Runs Through It, 5.10c, Gibraltar Rock
Danger Boy, 5.11a, Wheeler Gorge
Glory Days, 5.11c, Sespe Gorge

Best Traditional Routes

Tree Route, 5.5, Sespe Gorge
Mid-Face, 5.6R, Gibraltar Rock
Ending Crack, 5.7 PG13, Sespe Gorge
Lieback Annie, 5.7, Gibraltar Rock
Orangahang, 5.7, San Ysidro Canyon
Many Happy Returns, 5.9+, San Ysidro Canyon
Spontaneous Order, 5.10a, The Fortress
T-Crack, 5.10b, Gibraltar Rock
The Nose, 5.11a, Gibraltar Rock
Makunaima, 5.11b, Gibraltar Rock

Map Legend

══⟨101⟩══ US Highway	■ Building/Point of Interest
══⟨33⟩══ State Highway	⛺ Campground
─────── Local Road	❶ Climbing Area
═══════ Unpaved Road	Cliff Edge
------------ Trail	Crag/Boulder
∿ Small River or Creek	▲ Mountain Peak
⬭ Lake/Reservoir	🅿 Parking
▢ National Forest/Park	○ Town
▢ State/County Park	⊢──⊣ Tunnel

Ventura Overview

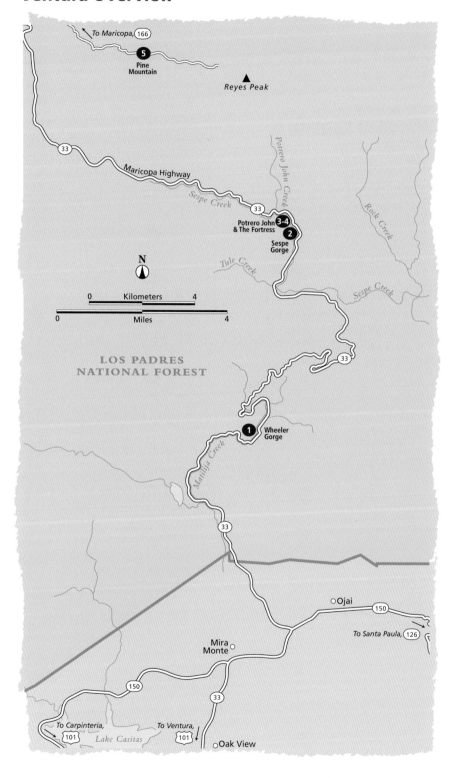

Ventura County

Ventura County gets overpassed by many climbers looking to get outside in the Santa Barbara region. Only a quick drive down the coast brings you to CA 33, aka the Maricopa Highway, which snakes for nearly 300 miles through Los Padres National Forest and into the San Joaquin Valley, ending just east of San Francisco. But for rock hounds on a hunt for amazing climbing, the journey on the 33 keeps you within 30 miles of the quaint town of Ojai. A total of five areas are featured in this guide, from excellent sport climbing in the narrow canyon of Wheeler Gorge, to multi-pitch traditional routes at Sespe Gorge, to perfect sandstone bouldering at the high elevations of Pine Mountain.

Sespe Gorge is the oldest recorded climbing area in Ventura County, dating back to Herb Rickert's ascent on the beginner's classic Tree Route (5.5) in the 1950s. This crag lies right on CA 33, a short trip from Ojai, and offers long traditional crack climbing deep in Los Padres National Forest. The Black Wall rises nearly 300 feet from the creek bed and dominates the landscape.

After the development of Sespe Gorge, Yvon Chouinard and Henry Barber were the first to climb at a small cliff just a half mile up the road, Potrero John. The first route was ascended in the 1970s up the center face using thin gear that Yvon was making during that time period. The area didn't get much more attention until the 1990s, when the routes were all re-bolted and cleaned up; now it is a great spot for beginners looking for a relaxing short wall.

Just a hop, skip, and a jump away from Potrero is one of the most unique areas in this book, The Fortress, a trio of shark fins seemingly plucked from some high-altitude peak in another land. The main peak dominates the landscape and demands attention when climbing—exposure and adventure are the name of the game here. It is thought the first climbing was done in the late 1960s, but little is known for sure. A spur of local development has occurred in the last decade, awakening this sleeping giant for climbers to enjoy.

It wasn't until the mid-1990s that a new area was developed: Wheeler Gorge. Just a few miles outside of Ojai, these steep to slabby walls offer a mixture of rock types and climbing styles. Some of the pioneers of that time were Steve Edwards, Reese Martin, Arvind Gupta, Stuart Ruckman, Tony Agulara, and Mike Gould. With such easy access—right next to the highway and close to town—this quickly became a popular spot for a day of well-equipped sport climbing.

The crown jewel of Ventura's CA 33 is Pine Mountain. It encompasses towering pine trees, perfectly placed campsites, crisp mountain air, epic views, and majestic sandstone boulders. This area was unknown for many years. Supposedly Yvon Chouinard ventured up here to "practice" for the big walls, but it wasn't until the mid-1990s that real development began. The bouldering here lends itself to beginner and moderate climbers, although a few more double-digit climbs have been ascended in the last few years.

The history in this region goes back to the Chumash Native Americans who inhabited the area over 13,000 years ago. The Chumash lived on the California coast for roughly 12,000 years, with their first settlements being on the Santa Barbara and Ventura coastlines. The Chumash were spread over 150 villages along the coast and specialized in bread making, herbalism, fishing, basketry, and rock art. You can still see traces of rock art at the Painted Caves in Santa Barbara.

The Wheeler Gorge Campground has lots of sites and can be found just past the Wheeler Gorge climbing area. Pine Mountain also has a large group campground and about eight other individual sites that are first-come, first-served; you must have a National Forest Adventure Pass to camp here. There is also camping just outside of Ojai at the Lake Casitas Recreation Area. With over 400 sites available, it can be busy and loud on the weekends. Check out www.casitaswater.org or call (805) 649-1122 for reservations.

A kite surfer finds the right wind stream on a gorgeous day down at C-Street at the Ventura Fairgrounds.

1.

Wheeler Gorge

Wheeler Gorge, just a short drive from the center of Ojai, is a great location for a short day of climbing. A quick walk from the car, Wheeler Gorge sits along a beautiful twisted canyon of the North Fork of Matilija Creek (ma-TILL-a-ha), where water has carved sheer cliffs into the mountains of Los Padres National Forest. A beautiful campground lies just past the climbing area and offers shady sites on a reservation basis. The creek runs right through the camp and has occasionally been stocked, making the trout

Wheeler Gorge

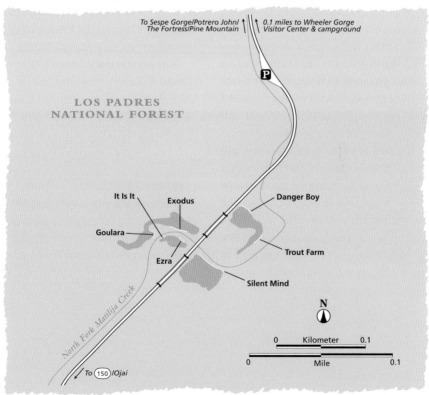

To Sespe Gorge/Potrero John/
The Fortress/Pine Mountain

0.1 miles to Wheeler Gorge
Visitor Center & campground

P

LOS PADRES
NATIONAL FOREST

It Is It
Exodus
Danger Boy

Goulara

Trout Farm

Ezra

Silent Mind

North Fork Matilija Creek

To 150/Ojai

N

0   Kilometer   0.1

0   Mile   0.1

fishing quite good. Wheeler essentially is a year-round crag: In the summer months you can escape the heat because the canyon is so narrow the sun doesn't heat it up as quickly as other locations; the fall and spring are perfect; and in the winter the temps can drop to the low 30s and 40s at certain parts of the day, perfect temps for sending that last project.

Development began in 1992 with Stuart Ruckman's ascent of the now popular greenschist route Stu Boy (5.9). In 1994 Mike Gould and Tony Agulara put up a handful of classic routes that were soon followed by major development in 1995 by Steve Edwards and Arvind Gupta. Development continues to this day. There are numerous well-protected beginner climbs that lead to softer climbs in the 5.10 range, making this area an ideal spot for a new leader to work his or her way up the grade scale with confidence.

After rainy days the rock can take some time to dry out, so be cautious and don't climb for a few days after rain. In addition, the creek can sometimes rise and make it difficult to access the start of a handful of routes.

Getting there: From US 101 drive north on CA 33 for 13.5 miles to the junction of CA 150 and CA 33 near the town of Ojai. Continue north on CA 33. You will drive through a tunnel after 7 miles (mile marker 18.23); two more tunnels follow another 0.5 mile down the road (mile marker 18.77). Just past the last tunnel is a pullout for gorge parking on the left-hand side of the road (mile marker 18.98).

Finding the crag: From the pullout on the left, walk back toward

Liza Butler laces up at the start of the climber's trail into the gorge.

Hjördis Rickert climbing Danger
Boy (5.11a), Wheeler Gorge

PHOTO BERND ZEUGSWETTER

Danger Boy Area

the last tunnel. If you plan on climbing at the "Stu Boy" wall, you can hop over the guardrail on the left, just before the entrance to the tunnel, and hike down to the creek to access these routes. If you plan on climbing anywhere else, it is best to hike through the tunnel and hop over the guardrail on the right just as you exit the tunnel.

DANGER BOY AREA

This is a great wall on some superb rock; the metamorphic greenschist lends to blockier edges on this tall wall.

Finding the crag: Depending on when you plan on climbing at this wall, you can access it two ways: by hopping over the guardrail on the left just before hiking through the first tunnel from the parking area, or by hopping over the guardrail on the right just after exiting the tunnel, then hiking alongside the creek past the Silent Mind area and Trout Farm wall. The wall is well equipped, and the routes are about 70 to 80 feet long with anchors, shuts, and chains.

Stuart's Rig (aka Stu Boy)

(5.9/5.11a) This route climbs up the right side of the arête to a large ledge you can rest on. From here the original line went up the dirty left gully, and this is the 5.9 escape

variation—be warned, it is very dirty. If you continue straight up toward a small roof, there is a great 5.11a crux involving a small, right-handed crimp over the roof. Another great variation from the ledge is to climb up the right-leaning crack (bring a small piece of gear for protection) to the anchors of Danger Boy and Velocity Boy; the climbing is only 5.9 through the crack. 7 bolts to chain anchors.

Danger Boy (5.11a) Danger Boy is the middle of the three routes and shares the same anchors as Velocity Boy. The rock on this route is amazing and should not be missed. After clipping the first bolt, you will encounter a reachy crux boulder problem, which is followed by easier 5.10 climbing up to and past a good ledge to rest. At the sixth bolt make a funky clip and then finish up one more bolt to the anchors. 7 bolts to 2 shared cold shuts.

Velocity Boy (5.11c) On the right side of the wall next to the concrete pillar is an arête that is technical and tricky to start, but once established on the wall, enjoyable climbing ensues up the arête to the large ledge, where you join up with Danger Boy and clip its final bolts. 7 bolts to 2 shared cold shuts.

TROUT FARM

The Trout Farm is a great wall to escape the crowds on busy days, and is an excellent place for a first-time leader—nice blocky edges follow a well-protected line up the wall.

Finding the crag: You can access this wall by following the creek to the left of the Danger Boy wall and walking around the bend; it is on the same side of the cliff as the previous wall. Or hike down at the end of the first tunnel from the parking area and follow the creek around the bend to the left.

South of the Trout Farm (5.9) This hidden gem features what almost seems like a fourth type of rock in this little canyon, as the sandstone here is very tightly packed and resembles granite. The first bolt is a bit high to start, but the climbing to get to it is the easiest on the route. The crux comes near the top, around the fourth bolt, and may feel more like 5.10a to some. 5 bolts to 2 cold shuts.

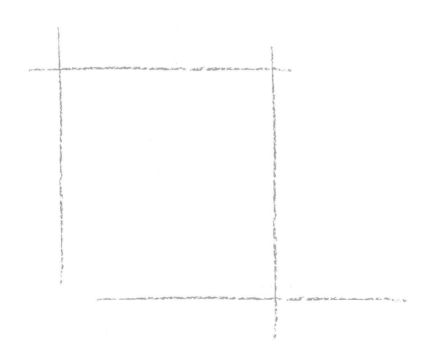

South of the
Trout Farm

SILENT MIND AREA

This area hosts a good mix of climbing from easy to hard on lots of cobbles. The left side of the cliff base stays dry most of the year, but Silent Mind (5.11b) and Aha! (5.11a) may be difficult to start in the wet season. Recent development has occurred here with the multi-pitch route Riparian Daydream (5.10-). The routes here range from 45 to 65 feet long with shuts at the top for anchors, with the exception of Riparian Daydream, which can be climbed just for the first pitch or the full three pitches.

Finding the crag: Access these routes by hiking to the left after hiking down from the bridge after the tunnel. The routes lie across the creek; you can cross where possible, depending on the water level.

Stolen from Mike (5.9+) This route is one of the newer additions to Wheeler Gorge, making this side of the wall a great place to set up topropes—and for beginners climbing their first outdoor routes. This is the second line of bolts in from the left side of the cobbled wall, starting below the overhang. Climb up into the overhang, which is much easier than it looks, and onto the low-angled section of the route, which proves to be the trickier part of this line. 5 bolts to 2 chain anchors.

Cobble Climb (5.8) If you are excited about climbing on actual cobbles, then this route is for you—it's a great toprope climb for beginners as well. The climbing begins at the large boulder at the base of the wall; climb up just below the overlap in the wall. Be cautious up to the second bolt—a fall from there won't be a painless one. Continue up the polished, low-angle wall to the top. 5 bolts to chain anchors.

Silent Mind Area

Cruiser (5.9) Another great route to sample some cobblestones. Some say this route is easier than Cobble Climb, but that might be because the crux comes early on this route (at the first little bulge) and it is well protected, something to consider if one of these routes is your first lead climb. The line starts just to the right of Cobble Climb, and the crux comes right off the bat with a long reach over the bulge. After this the climbing eases to 5.8 to join Cobble Climb's anchors. 5 bolts to chain anchors.

Riparian Daydream (5.10-) Another testament to vision and hard work for Wheeler Gorge, in autumn 2014 Alex Bury redpointed this masterpiece, rating it with a flexible 5.10- grade. If you don't have enough time to sample all three pitches, the first pitch features a 5.10- crux down low, with easier climbing through a short but steep 60 feet with five bolts protecting it to two ring anchors. Pitch 2 clocks in at 5.9+, with lots of ledges and blocky holds leading to a crux move at a roof below the exposed slab climbing above. Pitch 2 is 95 feet long with eight bolts and two ring anchors. It is safest to use a 70-meter rope for this pitch; if you only have a 60-meter line, be sure to knot the ends of the rope on the rappel, as you will reach the end of your line. The final pitch adds a rare opportunity to plug some gear at Wheeler Gorge—a short and steep section gets you to the base of a widening crack. Going from fingers

to hands, this crack will take three to four pieces up to the next crux at a small roof that is well protected with bolts. This pitch is 65 feet long with five bolts and cams ranging from 0.4 to 3 inches. As with any multi-pitch route, wearing a helmet will prevent injury from loose rocks.

Aha! (5.11a) Aha! is notoriously the hardest 5.11a in the gorge, but it is well worth the effort because the movement on this route is so much fun. There is a "starter rock" in the stream next to the wall, but depending on the season this rock may be well exposed or completely underwater. Climb up to the large horizontal crack at about 6 feet and traverse left to clip the first bolt. After clipping the second bolt, you will face the tricky crux move involving some thin crimps. After this crux the route joins Silent Mind for another four bolts, continuing up the face; there is a final crux to battle just below the anchors. Look for a thank-god jug just past the anchors from which to clip them. 6 bolts to 2 cold shuts.

Silent Mind (aka Steve's Rig) (5.11b) This is the direct start to Aha! From another set of "starter rocks" just to the right of Aha!, climb straight up to the overlap and use an undercling to gain the main headwall and cobbles. Climbing slightly to the left will get you to where this route and Aha! join up for the final four bolts and the last crux below the anchors. 6 bolts to 2 cold shuts.

EZRA AREA

This is one of the first walls you will notice when approaching the main area of the gorge. The beautiful line of cobbles draws the attention of all climbers as they arrive.

Finding the crag: This is one of the first climbs you will notice when hiking down after exiting the first tunnel from the parking area. Ezra sits right across the creek to the right of the bridge; you'll need to ford the creek where possible.

Ezra (5.9) A great route for beginners. Well-protected climbing leads up this cobbled wall for 45 feet. If you have never climbed on cobbles and you are curious to see what all the rage is about, this may be a good route to start with. Only four bolts long and closely bolted, the route draws lots of newbies to its base. Many cobbles have fallen out of their cavities over the years, so the route is a mixture of smooth cobbles and deep, round holes. Enjoy the ride up this short cruise. 4 bolts to 2 bolt anchors.

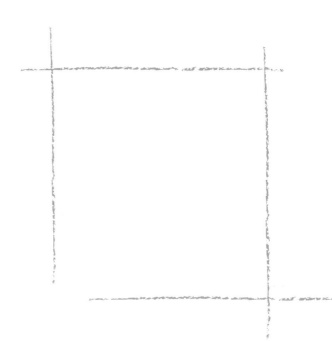

Ezra

EXODUS AREA

This wall boasts some excellent slab climbing on great hardpacked, gray coastal sandstone. Of all the Wheeler Gorge walls, Exodus gets the most sun throughout the day, and it is easily accessible.

Finding the crag: After hiking through the first tunnel from the parking area, hop over the guardrail on the right, hike down to the creek, and follow it to the right; soon you can access the lower slabs and climb up to the base of the routes on your right. You can also stay at road level after hopping the guardrail and follow the cliff band to the right to access the routes. The routes here are 60 to 80 feet long.

Gridlock (5.10a) The easiest route on this finely compacted gray wall was one of the more recent additions by Erik and Crystal Anderson in the summer of 2012. Start below the large triangular roof and climb 20 feet of slab to the first bolt at the overhang. After clipping the first bolt, climb to the left toward a large knob. From here the climb trends to the left a little more while following a black water streak to the anchors. The first bolt is a little runout; adding a 1-inch and a 3-inch cam will

Exodus Area

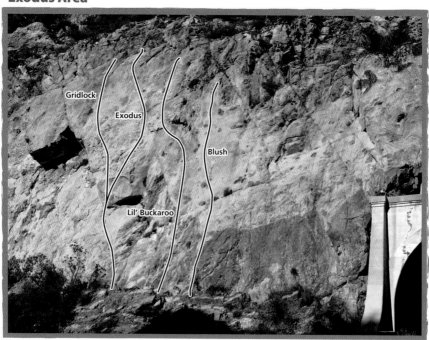

protect the start better. 5 bolts to 2 ring anchors.

Exodus (5.11a) Exodus shares the same start as Gridlock but splits right after the first bolt. After clipping the second bolt, continue climbing slightly to the right for two more bolts until you reach a thin seam, then climb up and left for four more bolts to the anchors. The last bit is slightly easier if you climb straight to the anchor through a small corner after the seventh bolt. The first bolt is a little runout; adding a 1-inch and a 3-inch cam will protect the start better. 8 bolts to chain anchors.

Lil' Buckaroo (5.11a) The next line of bolts to the right of Exodus offers some technical and sustained slab climbing up to a large, left-curving roof. Start up the slab where you quickly encounter small crimps getting past the second bolt. From here follow seven more bolts up to the left as you stay under the arching roof. 9 bolts to cold shuts.

Blush (5.10d) This route is the next line of bolts a few feet to the right of Lil' Buckaroo. Climb up the initial slab for two bolts, then trend to the left a little to the crux at the fourth bolt. Moving to the large holds on the left of the bolt is slightly easier than the small crimps on the right. Follow two more bolts to the anchors. 6 bolts to 2 bolt anchors.

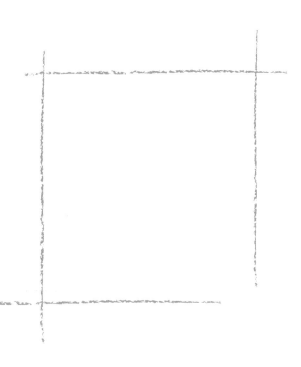

GOULARA AREA

This area rests in the westernmost end of the canyon where the creek makes a sharp left turn. A handful of excellent climbs are in this corner, and the climbing is on well-established cobbles. The area is best known for Goulara (5.10c/5.11+), a stunning face or arête route put up in 1995 by Mike Gould and Tony Agulara.

Finding the crag: After hiking through the first tunnel from the parking area and hopping over the guardrail on the right, hike down to the creek and follow it to the right to where the creek takes a sharp bend to the left. Goulara and Economique (5.10a) are located on the right side of the creek. It Is It sits at the bend on the left side of the creek. Goulara and Economique are 70 to 80 feet tall.

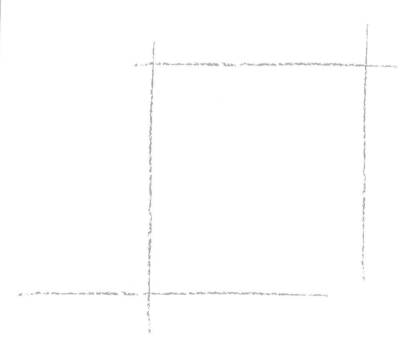

Andy Patterson climbing
the direct finish to Goulara
(5.10c/5.11+), Wheeler Gorge
PHOTO BERND ZEUGSWETTER

It Is It (5.12b) This is a great route for boulderers—short, sweet, and to the point. As you're walking toward Goulara, the creek takes a sharp left; at this bend, on the opposite side of the creek, is the start to this route. Begin on a stone that is sometimes submerged at the base of the route and climb straight up on slick rock to the first bolt, then make some bouldery moves right, to the second bolt located inside a large black xeno. Continue with sustained climbing to the anchors. 4 bolts to cold shuts.

Points of Interest and History
Wheeler Gorge is blessed with three types of rock, varying from water-worn conglomerate to coastal sandstone to metamorphic greenschist. You can see each one represented, respectively, on the Goulara wall, Exodus wall, and Stu Boy wall.

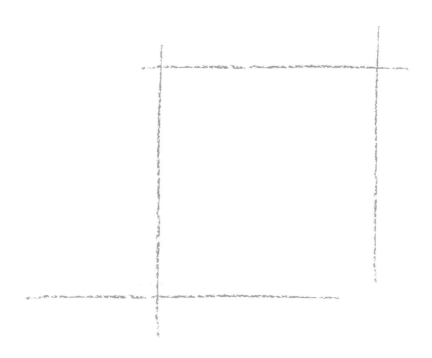

It Is It

Goulara (5.10c/5.11+) This route has seen a lot of controversy in recent years due to extra bolts being added to the original line; luckily local developers have kept an eye on things and are trying to keep the original route in place. The first bolt is a runout 5.10a move, so bring a stick clip or a 2-inch cam to protect the opening crack. Continue up four more bolts to the arête. From here the climbing is 5.10c if you use the arête and make the long reaches to the right to clip the last three bolts to the anchor. If you climb onto the face away from the arête to clip the last three bolts, it is a very technical and thought-provoking 5.11+ face climb. 8 bolts to a 3-bolt anchor.

Economique (5.10a) This is known as one of the best 5.10a routes around, with great arête climbing and exposure adding to the pleasurable route. Start the same as for Goulara, using a stick clip for the first bolt or protecting the opening crack with a 2-inch cam, then climb the next three bolts and arrive at the arête. Climb around to the left side of the arête onto the face and clip four more bolts on your way to the anchors. Enjoy the view! 7 bolts to bolt anchors.

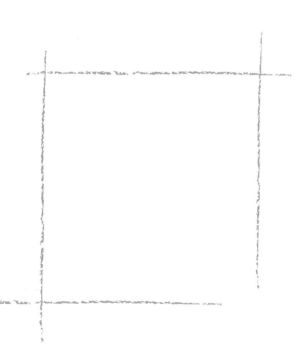

Sespe Gorge

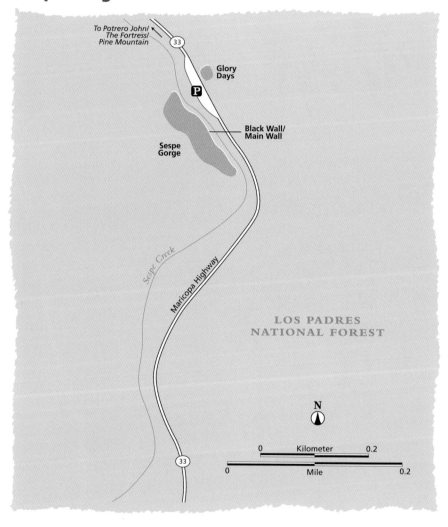

To Potrero John/
The Fortress/
Pine Mountain

33

Glory
Days

P

Black Wall/
Main Wall

Sespe
Gorge

Sespe Creek

Maricopa Highway

LOS PADRES
NATIONAL FOREST

N

33

0   Kilometer   0.2
0   Mile   0.2

2.

Sespe Gorge

Sespe Gorge has long, easy, multi-pitch climbing on sandstone cracks, which is a rare gem for the coast. The wall here reaches heights of 300 feet at its tallest point, all just off the side of the roadway. This crag is where Herb Rickert ascended the first climbs on lead in Ventura County in the 1950s. The region didn't get much attention for some time, until Yvon Chouinard moved to Ventura and brought his young climbing equipment company, Chouinard Equipment Ltd., along with a ton of fresh and talented rock climbers. Soon enough, in the mid-1960s Yvon and his crew slowly started ticking off the gems along the walls at Sespe Gorge. Yvon, Dick Blankenbecler, and William Thompson continued to develop Sespe Gorge well into the 1970s, establishing such local classics as Slime Climb (5.3), Mrs. Murphy's Old Packard (5.5), Pipe Prime (5.6), Leaning Tower (5.5), Rottenrete (5.4), and Wadka (5.7). None of these routes stand out individually as a five-star "classic," but they are worth the mention because they started the movement in the Ventura region. The routes listed in this guide have stood the test of time and you can still find

Two climbers on the Main Wall at Sespe Gorge on a sunny day in Los Padres National Forest
PHOTO MATTHEW FIENUP

An aquatic, two-striped garter snake *(Thamnophis hammondii)* in the stream at the base of the Main Wall
Photo Matthew Fienup

a line at the base of the wall on a perfect weekend.

Getting there: From US 101 drive north on CA 33 for 13.5 miles to the junction of CA 150 and CA 33 near the town of Ojai. Continue north on CA 33 for 20 miles; look for a sign for mile marker 31.18. The Black Wall at Sespe Gorge will be on your left and is hard to miss; find parking just off the highway in dirt pullouts.

Finding the crags: From the highway walk directly toward the cliff; there are small climber's trails leading across the creek and to the base of the Black Wall. The Glory Days block is on the opposite side of the highway from the Black Wall.

THE BLACK WALL

This is the highlight of the area—the oldest known routes in Ventura are on this 300-foot-tall sandstone cliff. Be careful with loose blocks and vegetation; in wet years the vegetation can grow back quickly and small rocks can get loosened. Most routes can be led to the summit, but the final pitches are not all worth mentioning in this book. The pitches are long, so a 70-meter rope is required, and two ropes should be used for rappels, or you can walk off the backside to descend the left part of the wall.

Finding the crag: Follow the small climber's trails that lead across the creek and to the base of the Black Wall. Routes are listed from left to right.

The Black Wall Left Side

Lost in the Sespe (5.7+ PG13) One of the more recent additions to the Black Wall, located on the far left side of the wall directly beneath a large roof on the wall above. Begin just to the left of two pipes and climb up left through the face toward a small pine tree. From here continue straight up toward a series of right-facing flakes and the large corner above. Climb along the corner and around to a nice belay ledge. One more easy pitch leads to the summit. The route is about 265 feet; use a 70-meter rope. **Rack:** Double rack from 0.25 to 3 inches (a couple larger pieces will come in handy), lots of slings to reduce rope drag. **Descent:** Walk off the backside.

Half Ascent (5.6R) Start underneath the large roof on the wall and climb up through a series of left-leaning crack systems. As you approach the roof, climb to the left side of it to a tree where you can build an anchor.

The first pitch is about 120 feet long. The second pitch takes you to the summit, but is not the best quality. **Rack:** Standard rack from 0.5 to 3 inches. **Descent:** Use two 70-meter ropes to descend.

Chip's Block (5.6) For the first pitch, start to the right of Half Ascent and climb along a nice left-leaning crack that takes limited gear to the base of the major right-facing corner on the wall; build an anchor here. The second pitch follows the corner up and to the right until you can climb around it and onto a belay ledge. It may be tricky to build an anchor here, but it is possible. You can scramble to the left and into a gully down to the rappel tree for Half Ascent. The route is about 250 feet. **Rack:** Standard rack from 0.25 to 3.5 inches.

Slime Climb (5.3) This climb begins in a crack to the right of a steel platform. Climb up toward some small bushes on a ledge, then continue up a left-leaning crack that can stay damp after rain. Continue through the second pitch toward the summit. **Rack:** Standard rack up to 3 inches. **Descent:** Walk off the back ridge or rappel from the top of Half Ascent.

The Wasp (5.8) This line starts in the alcove next to the metal platform. Climb up the crack and flake system on the left side of the alcove to the main wall, where you will find some huecos with slings from which to belay or lower off here. For the second pitch, continue up the right-trending crack toward some large bushes where you can build a belay station. From here traverse to the left of the bushes and continue straight up the crack toward the large roof near the summit. You can climb straight through the roof or around to the left. **Rack:** Standard rack up to 4 inches and extra slings. **Descent:** Walk off the back ridge or scramble around to the right and descend the 4th-class gully.

The Sting (5.10+ R) Start in the same alcove as The Wasp but climb up the center on face holds toward the hand jams over the lip of the cave. You will have to sling a horn as protection in the alcove and use a 2-inch cam as backup just below the horn. You can rappel from the top of the alcove from some slung huecos, or continue up the last two pitches of The Wasp.

Pipe Cleaner (5.6) This route starts about 50 feet to the right of the metal platform where The Sting and The Wasp start. Climb up the major crack that fluctuates between wide and narrow, sometimes turning into a semi-corner as it leads to a 2-bolt anchor at the top of the wall. **Rack:** Standard rack up to 3 inches. **Descent:** The route is 160 feet and takes two ropes to rappel; you can also scramble down the 4th-class gully to the left.

The Black Wall Right Side

White Spider (5.7R) Ascend the next major crack to the right of Pipe Cleaner. Bring some thin gear for the crack as you head up to a 2-bolt anchor. **Rack:** Standard rack with extra small gear. **Descent:** The route is 160 feet, so use two ropes to rappel, or scramble down the 4th-class gully on the left.

Ending Crack (5.7 PG13) This is one of the most popular routes at the wall. Climb up the perfect hand crack just to the right of White Spider to an excellent two-bolt hanging belay. The first pitch is great for beginners, who may want to stop here; the second pitch gets a bit harder when the crack peters out and the gear gets slim. At this point climb to the right on some face holds and another crack to a 3-bolt anchor at the top. **Rack:** Standard rack up to 3 inches. **Descent:** Scramble down the gully on the left or make a two-rope, 300-foot rappel.

Tree Route (5.5) The start of this route is next to a large tree just two major crack systems to the right of Ending Crack. You may have to wait in line for this plumb line, but it's worth it. Climb up and left on the bomber crack that takes mostly small gear for the first pitch to a set of bolts for a hanging belay next to a tree. You can rappel on a single 70-meter rope from here or continue up pitch 2. The second pitch heads into a wider crack that leads slightly to the right, passing many small trees along the way for protection. The climb shares the anchors for Ending Crack. **Rack:** Standard rack up to 3 inches, lots of slings for trees. **Descent:** Scramble down the 4th-class gully to the left or make a two-rope, 300-foot rappel.

Pine to Pine (5.6) If you are looking for a long, old-school adventure route, then look no further. Most likely this was one of the earlier routes led on the wall with pitons. Begin just to the right of Tree Route at the base of a large pine tree and climb up the disconnected crack system toward another large tree at the top of the wall for two pitches. Be prepared to route find. **Rack:** Standard rack up to 3 inches. **Descent:** Make a two-rope rappel.

With beautiful fall colors and perfect fall temps, Bryson Fienup enjoys Tree Route at Sespe Gorge. PHOTO MATTHEW FIENUP

Edge of Night (5.7R) On the far right side of the wall is a striking arête on the edge of a gully. Start the first pitch by climbing up the arête (gear is far apart and few between on the horizontal cracks). You can build a belay anchor at the tree in the gully; from here the climbing gets a lot more exposed on better rock to the summit. The route is about 200 feet long, and there is a 2-bolt anchor at the top of the second pitch. **Rack:** Standard rack up to 3 inches.

Points of Interest and History
The earliest recorded ascent in the Ventura County region is Tree Route (5.5) and Pine to Pine (5.6) at Sespe Gorge in the late 1950s by Herb Rickert.

Along with Yvon Chouinard, world-class surfer Bob McTavish from Australia helped develop the classic 5.6 route McTavish. Bob was one of the great surfers and board shapers in the 1960 to 1970 surf movement across the globe.

Black Wall

Edge of Night

GLORY DAYS

This solitary boulder across the highway from the main cliff boasts one excellent route and some projects. The main line up the wall is the hardest at the crag, coming in at 5.11c.

Finding the crag: The Glory Days block is on the opposite side of the highway from the Black Wall, next to the pullout parking.

Glory Days (5.11c) Start with a run and jump to the first hueco on the wall. From here clip the first bolt and make a dynamic move up and right to the next hueco. Continue up and left with some dynamic moves, depending on your height, to easier climbing. 4 bolts to a 2-bolt anchor.

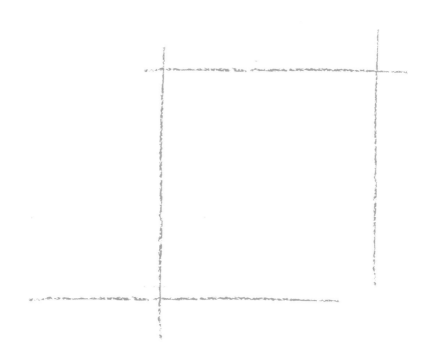

Glory Days

Glory Days

Potrero John/The Fortress

LOS PADRES
NATIONAL FOREST

Derry Dale Creek

Sespe Creek

Potrero John

The Fortress

To Sespe Gorge/Wheeler Gorge & 150

33

Potrero John Creek

Sespe Creek

To Pine Mountain

33

N

Kilometer
0   0.2

Mile
0   0.2

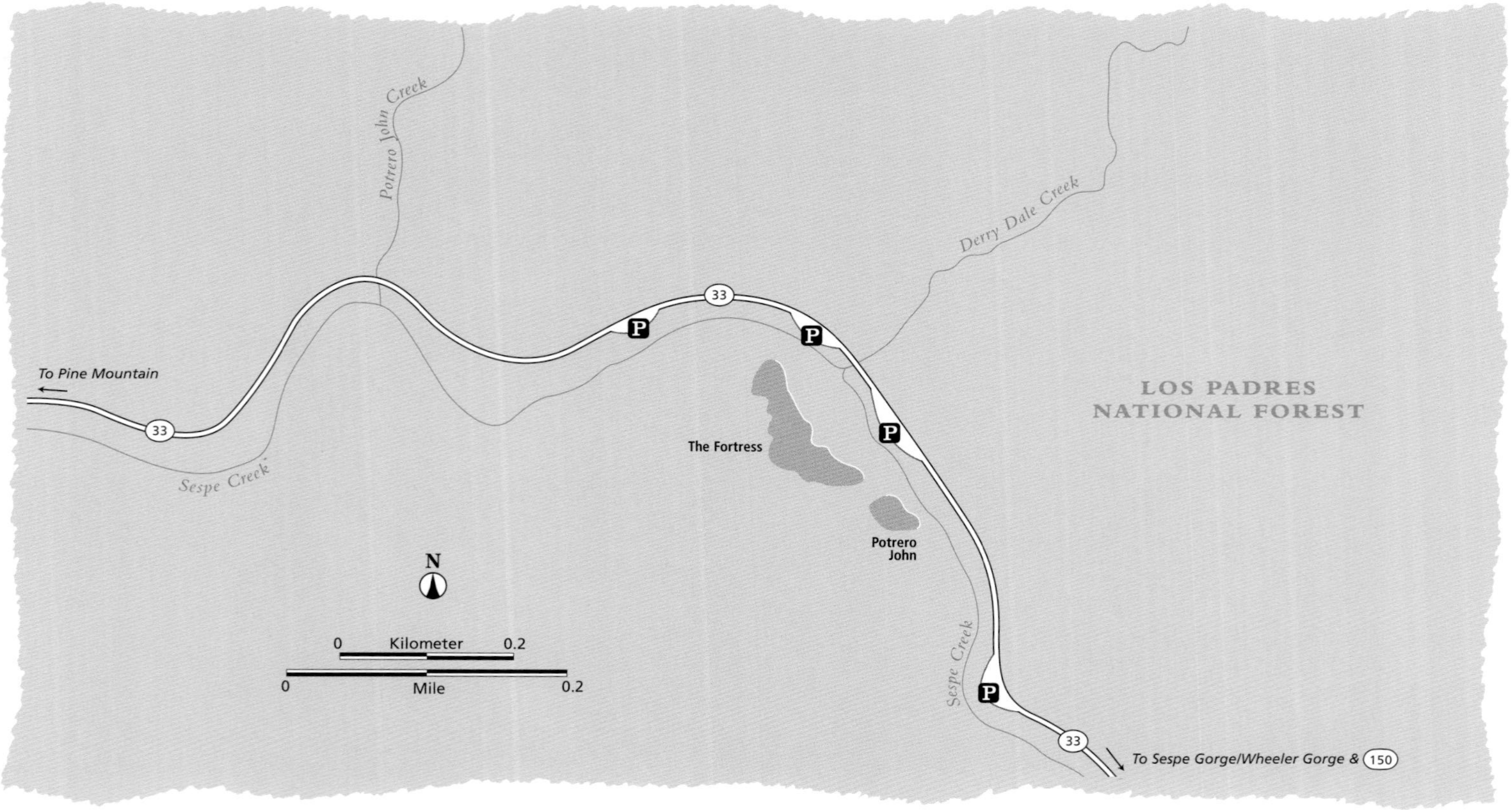

3.

Potrero John

Potrero John is a great little sport-bolted crag just up the road from Sespe Gorge, and was most likely developed as the answer to the traditional routes found at Sespe. The earliest recorded ascents can be traced back to Yvon Chouinard and Henry Barber climbing the thin seam up the middle of the wall, most likely a great testing ground for some of Yvon's new gear he was making. It wasn't until the mid-1990s that Reese Martin came in and re-bolted many of the older bolts placed along the wall. In the late 1990s Matt Polk and Dan Frame added a couple of newer lines, rounding this area out to a good half-day crag.

Nothing here is harder than 5.10 and the wall is only about 80 feet tall, a great spot for beginners or just a relaxing day to get some laps in. Just upstream from the small crag are some great swimming opportunities for hot summer days, as long as the stream is running.

Potrero John/Main Wall

Getting there: From US 101 drive north on CA 33 for 13.5 miles to the junction of CA 150 and CA 33 near the town of Ojai. Continue north on CA 33 for 20.5 miles (mile marker 31.60); the crag will be on your left, and it may be hidden from the road behind some trees, depending on the season. Parking is available in dirt pullouts on the left or right side of the road.

Finding the crag: From the parking, follow the small climber's trails down to the creek and cross the creek where possible. The crag is located to the left about 200 feet after finding a good crossing.

POTRERO JOHN MAIN WALL

This is the main climbing wall, where the routes are vertical and full of edges and pockets. Most routes here are only 60 to 80 feet long and have four to seven bolts, depending on which side of the wall you are on.

Should I Go (aka El Potrero) (5.10b) There are two routes on the far left side of the wall—both were bolted in the late 1990s and come in around 5.10b. Choose the left or right set of bolts and climb up thin edges to easier climbing near the top. 5 bolts to a 2-bolt anchor.

Migrating Coconuts (aka Zyzzxx) (5.9) A perfect route to start the day on: great rock, great moves, and well protected. This is the line of bolts a few feet to the left of the huge hueco at the base of the wall. The crux comes around the third bolt, then climbing eases up to the top. You can set up topropes easily for all the other lines by climbing this route. 5 bolts to a 2-bolt anchor.

Pro Job (5.9) Start in the right side of the large hueco at the base of the wall and climb up through one bolt, then traverse to the right to join up

The yellow sorrel blooms in San Ysidro Canyon during the springtime.

with Miccis at its second bolt. Continue up the face using pockets and good edges to the anchor. 4 bolts to a 2-bolt anchor.

Miccis (5.9) This is the original direct line of Pro Job. Miccis features great rock for its entirety, with positive edges in between long reaches and pockets. 4 bolts to a 2-bolt anchor.

Ménage à Trois (5.10b) The original line on the wall, this route was climbed by Yvon Chouinard and Henry Barber in 1976 using only tiny wired Stoppers in the thin seam and EBs for shoes. Now this route is bolted for the everyday climber to enjoy, but it is nice to follow in the footsteps of such legends. Small gear or Tricams will help the initial runout between the first two bolts. 4 bolts to 2 bolt anchors.

Rubber Man (aka Color Blind) (5.10d) Just to the right of Ménage à Trois's thin seam is possibly the hardest route at the crag. Great rock leads to a tricky undercling/roof crux past the first bolt. From here sustained climbing on small features leads to the redpoint crux just after the fifth bolt. 6 bolts to 2 bolt anchors.

> **Points of Interest and History**
> The route named Migrating Coconuts came from a Monty Python reference from the *Quest for the Holy Grail,* which goes to show how clever we climbers can be.

Cleaning Lady (5.10c) This route and Rubber Man were the most recent additions to the crag in the late 1990s, so the rock here is a little sharper and stickier than the routes on the left and center of the wall. This route starts on the far right side of the wall underneath the large pine tree. Climb up through a right-leaning seam to a very beta-intensive and tricky crux up high, followed by sustained climbing to the anchors. 7 bolts to 2 bolt anchors.

Beginnings (5.5 TR) No topo. Just to the right of the main Potrero John wall is a separate rock with an easy traditional climb on it. A standard rack ranging from 0.5 to 3 inches will suffice for this weaving and varied crack. Bring long slings for an anchor. **Descent:** You can walk off the left side of the route or follow the slabs back down to the right.

Romain Wacziarg on the stunning last pitch of Permanent Income Hypothesis (5.9), The Fortress

4.

The Fortress

This stunning crag boasts some of the most adventurous multi-pitch traditional routes around; it's a wonder why this took so long to get heavily developed and documented. A trio of breathtaking triangular summits forms the main body of The Fortress, and once you get to the base of the wall, you will notice many smaller formations with excellent route potential. A majority of the climbing occurs on the three main peaks.

The earliest known history seems to date to the late 1960s and then nothing more until the early 1980s. Unfortunately nothing was recorded back then, so it is uncertain what lines were climbed and when. It wasn't until recently, with the help of Matthew Fienup, Romain Wacziarg, and Jesse Groves and crew, that the area began to get noticed again in the late 2000s. The team helped to clean up and safely protect the most stunning and obvious lines, and there is still much potential at The Fortress. Be sure to bring your adventure hat when visiting this crag, as lots of route finding is necessary to approach each route. A standard rack and some extra-long slings will come in handy as well as a helmet—there are still a lot of sections that are slightly loose. Many of the routes are rope stretchers, so bring two ropes and make smart rappel decisions.

Getting there: From US 101 drive north on CA 33 for 13.5 miles to the junction of CA 150 and CA 33 near the town of Ojai. Continue north on CA 33 for 20.5 miles; the crag is on your left just 0.5 mile past Sespe Gorge. The main formation towers above the road and is unmistakable with its three triangular peaks. Parking is available in a dirt pullout on the left, just past Derry Dale Creek Bridge, with mile marker 31.72 on it.

Finding the crag: From the parking, follow small climber's trails down to the creek and cross the creek where possible. The crag is located to the right or left after finding a good creek crossing, depending on where you walked in.

CENTRAL GULLY

The Central Gully is lower angled than the right gully and hosts the more moderate routes of the area. This is most likely where some of the earliest ascents occurred. If you are looking for a great all-day adventure, you can combine four single pitches with some scrambling in between to climb Spontaneous Order (5.10a R), which is the link-up of four separate routes.

Finding the crag: Follow the directions from the parking area; the Central Gully is the major gully on the left side of The Fortress. Climb Footprints to access all the listed routes.

Spontaneous Order (5.10a R) This is a link-up of the following routes: Footprints, Blue in Green, Rational Expectations, and Seven Steps to Heaven. See individual route descriptions.

Footprints (5.4) This is the main approach route for any of the lines going up the Central Gully. Start at the base of the slabs with a well-protected crux at the bottom leading into easier 4th- and 5th-class climbing. 4 bolts to 2 bolt anchors.

Snickerdoodle (5.9) From the top of Footprints, you have to walk/scramble to the left for roughly 100 feet past a gully to access the base of this rounded arête. Climb up on easy terrain to start, staying on the arête. At the fourth bolt it is 5.9 if you continue climbing to the left of the bolts; if you stay on the actual arête to the right of the bolts, the climb will feel more like 5.10a. 100 feet, 8 bolts to a 2-bolt anchor and rings. **Descent:** You can make a 30-foot rappel to the right of the route to access Lunch Ledge and the routes that begin there; otherwise rappel back down through the gully to the top of Footprints.

Blue in Green (5.6) This route begins to the right and above the anchors for Footprints. Start climbing up the slab past three bolts, where you may want to place a 2-inch cam just below the pine tree, or sling the tree itself as you pass it on your left. Climb up and slightly to the left past three more bolts to the top anchors at Lunch Ledge. 110 feet, 6 bolts to 2 bolt anchors. **Descent:** Rappel the route using two ropes, or rappel the gully on the route's left back to the anchors of Footprints.

Rational Expectations (5.7) This route starts at Lunch Ledge where Blue in Green's anchor is located. Climb the left side of the formation on positive edges up the exposed face. You may want to supplement the bolt placements with some medium Stoppers. 4 bolts to 2 bolt anchors. **Descent:** Rappel the route, and then rappel into the gully between Snickerdoodle and Blue in Green to the anchors of Footprints.

Magali's Arête (5.8) From the top of Lunch Ledge, climb the arête on the right side of the formation, a slightly harder and longer route than Rational Expectations. Start up a short slab to access the main wall, and then follow the featured arête up to the anchor. You may want an extra 2-inch cam. 5 bolts to a 2-bolt anchor with chains.

Seven Steps to Heaven (5.10a) For an outstanding experience, be

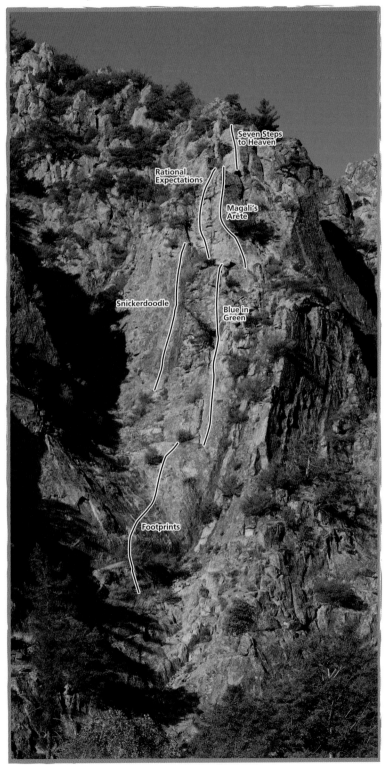

Imprint of brittle stars, found in The Fortress at an elevation of 4,000 feet above sea level
PHOTO MATTHEW FIENUP

sure to check out this route. Way at the top of the Central Gully is an unmatched summit block that is rarely seen in this region. To access this route, you must climb either Rational Expectations or Magali's Arête. Climb just to the left of the sharp arête to gain the summit block. 4 bolts to a 2-bolt anchor with rings.

RIGHT SIDE GULLY

The Right Side Gully boasts the most aesthetic lines at the crag with its towering arêtes. Climbing on these arêtes gives you the feel of wildness and altitude with lots of exposure. Be prepared to route find and bring a helmet. Many of the pitches are long, so two ropes can be helpful but are not necessary; pay attention to your rappel points.

Finding the crag: The best way to access the Right Side Gully is to park at the major dirt pullout before the highway takes a wide left turn. From here walk toward the creek bed, where you will find places to cross, then walk left toward the base of the wall looking for a boulder-filled drainage—the start of

Permanent Income Hypothesis can be found here.

Natural Rate of Unemployment
(5.10c) This route climbs up the center of the main face in the gully; the start is just to the left of Capitalism & Freedom. To access this route you must climb the first pitch of Free to Choose and traverse 2nd-class terrain to the left past the starts to two other routes. Climb up the center of the face on good edges and flakes to a crux at the halfway point, around the seventh bolt, then finish up easier terrain to a pine tree at the top where you will find the anchors just off to

> **Points of Interest and History**
> On the way to Ojai, you pass through a small town named Casitas Springs. Johnny Cash called this place his home in the early 1960s; during his time here one of his most famous songs was blazing across the country—"Ring of Fire."

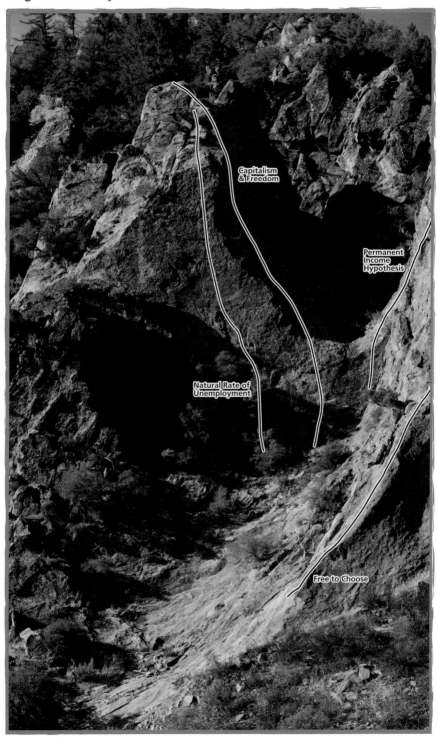

the right. 115 feet, 13 bolts to 2 bolt anchors with rings. **Descent:** If you have a 70-meter rope, it is possible to rappel the route from here; if you have a shorter rope, continue climbing another 15 feet to the anchors of Capitalism & Freedom, where you can do two rappels from there back to the gully and then retrace your steps to the anchors of Free to Choose.

Capitalism & Freedom (5.10b) This two-pitch route starts a few feet to the left of the start of Permanent Income Hypothesis. Access this route by climbing the first pitch of Free to Choose and traversing to the left through 2nd-class terrain. The first pitch holds the route's crux early on, at the second bolt; continue on good edges for another three bolts. 80 feet long, 5 bolts to a 2-bolt anchor. The second pitch is only 5.9 but gets a little runout and exposed, and you may want to bring a couple of 1- to 1.5-inch cams for a crack to protect the crux just above the fifth bolt. This adventurous pitch will reward you with one of the best views around. 85 feet, 8 bolts to 2 bolt anchors. **Descent:** Rappel the route in two lengths, then retrace your steps back to the top of Free to Choose. It is possible to stretch this route into one pitch with a 60-meter rope.

Permanent Income Hypothesis (5.9) This has to be the area classic for sure—it's the most striking arête and the route leads to the most airy and wild final 40 feet to a stunning summit block. To access the base of the route, you must climb the first pitch of Free to Choose. From the anchors you can unclip and traverse easy 2nd-class terrain along a ledge to the left for 80 feet. You will be faced with the crux climbing past the first bolt; from here the climbing stays 5.8 all the way to the top arête. 180 feet, 16 bolts to 2 bolt anchors with chains. **Descent:** Rappel off the chains to the right side of the formation, then rappel down 90 feet into the gully to a grassy ledge where you will find another set of bolts. From here you can rappel back to the base of the route and then retrace your steps back to the anchors of Free to Choose.

Free to Choose (5.7) This route is the stunning, long arête that flows up the left side of the formation. Start at the bottom of the long, slabby apron of rock at the base of the arête and climb up through the well-protected, 3-foot-wide arête. The last bolt leads off to the left, and the last few moves entail crossing over the gully to clip the anchors. Typically this route is climbed as one pitch to the first set of anchors and used as a jumping-off point for the other routes in the Right Side Gully. 95 feet, 9 bolts to 2 bolt anchors. Feel "Free to Choose" if you want to continue for an adventurous second pitch. Pitch 2 is 85 feet long with eight bolts, finishing with a dihedral and clocking in around 5.9. Be cautious with loose rock up here. **Descent:** You can rappel each pitch.

Right Side Gully

Right Side Gully

Consumption Dysfunction (5.9+) This and the next route are located on the triangular "flatiron" on the far right side of The Fortress. You will have to scramble up to the base of the climb; this route is the left set of bolts. It's the less popular of the two routes here, but is worth a mention because it is quite a bit easier. Start just to the left of a tree and climb through a faint water streak up to the steeper headwall above. Finish up by climbing to the left of a bush just before the anchors. 75 feet, 7 bolts to 2 open shuts.

Classically Liberal (5.11a) If you are looking for more of a challenge at The Fortress, hop on this route and expect lots of pinches and sidepulls between dynamic and steep climbing. Follow the same directions as Consumption Dysfunction to access the base of this climb; it is the right-most line of bolts that starts just to the right of the tree at the base of the wall. The crux is technical and comes early getting to the second bolt; from here, with the proper sequence, the climbing eases to about 5.9. You may want to supplement your rack with a 1- or 2-inch cam to protect the last few moves to the anchors. 75 feet, 6 bolts to 2 open shuts.

5.

Pine Mountain

One of the most stunning and far-reaching bouldering areas in all of Southern California, Pine Mountain is a true destination for anyone coming to the region. Near the summit of Reyes Peak lies an idyllic forest at 7,000 feet in elevation, with towering jeffrey, sugar, and little ponderosa pines among beautiful red-hued sandstone boulders. There are excellent camping options along the forest road—some sites with picnic tables and campfire rings and some nestled in between climbable boulders; sites are free but require a National Forest Adventure Pass. There is one large group-style camping/picnic area with six sites, and about eight other small sites along the ridgeline.

The first recorded history of bouldering here was in the mid-1990s; it was around this time that Reese Martin, Steve Edwards, and Wills Young all began ticking off the gems. Pine Mountain was featured in a couple of magazine articles and mini guides in the late 1990s, but was never put on the map as a major bouldering destination. This allowed Pine Mountain to retain its secluded feel along with its untapped ridgeline of boulders—the surface has merely been scratched

Timmy Nelson runs a second lap on a hidden gem on a crisp fall morning at Pine Mountain, The Choadler, V4.

Group Campsite/Picnic Area

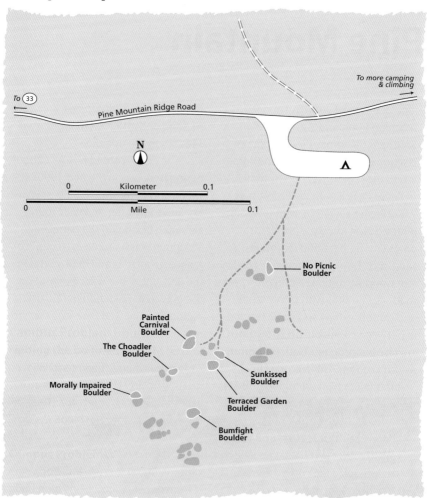

To more camping & climbing →

To (33) ←

Pine Mountain Ridge Road

N

| 0 | Kilometer | 0.1 |
| 0 | Mile | 0.1 |

No Picnic Boulder

Painted Carnival Boulder

The Choadler Boulder

Sunkissed Boulder

Morally Impaired Boulder

Terraced Garden Boulder

Bumfight Boulder

here. Pine Mountain is the beginner and moderate climber's dream; most climbs range from VB to V6, with only a handful of climbs reaching double digits until recently. Nonetheless, it has always attracted strong climbers, even to the point where a bouldering competition, the Pine Mountain Pull Down, was held here in the late 2000s. The service road to the campground closes in the winter; call the local ranger station (805-646-4348) for updates when spring returns.

Getting there: From US 101 drive north on CA 33 for 13.5 miles to the junction of CA 150 and CA 33 near the town of Ojai. Continue north on CA 33 for 31.5 miles to a fire road on the right just past a large sign on the right for the campground (mile marker 42.73). Take the Pine Mountain Ridge Road for 4.8 miles to reach the Group Campsite and Picnic Area, then continue 1 more mile to reach the main Reyes Peak campground and the rest of the climbing. See specific directions for each area.

GROUP CAMPSITE/PICNIC AREA

Finding the boulders: The Picnic Area is the first area you come to, 4.8 miles after leaving CA 33. Look for a large camping and picnic area on your right and park here. The boulders are up the hill directly in front of you as you drive into the large pullout; follow the right fork on the walking trails.

No Picnic Boulder
Finding the boulder: This is the first boulder you will see on your way up the hill, on your left.

Picnic (V1) Start low on big holds on the far left side of the boulder, make a big move with the right hand, and then follow the arête to the top and more jugs.

Picnic Eliminate (V4) Start in the middle of the wall on a good hold in the hueco, then make a huge dyno to a giant jug at the lip straight up.

No Picnic (V4) Start as for Picnic Eliminate and move right to a gaston in a dish, then move up using a sloper on the way to the top.

No Picnic Boulder

Sunkissed Boulder

Finding the boulder: A little farther up the trail from the No Picnic Boulder is this boulder on your left.

Sunkissed (V0) Start this route on the right side of the wall at the crack; climb up on good holds and onto the blunt arête to the top.

Lelah's Traverse (V0) Begin at Sunkissed but then traverse to the left along a sloping shelf for a couple moves until you get to more jugs heading up and left to top out.

Juan Carlo Dyno (V1) Start in the middle of the wall at the sloping shelf and dyno to the top. You can also traverse in from Sunkissed and do the dyno.

Sunkissed Boulder

Sunkissed

Lelah's Traverse

Juan Carlo Dyno

Terraced Garden Boulder

Finding the boulder: This boulder sits right behind Sunkissed Boulder.

Terraced Garden (V0) Climb up the tall right side of the boulder using the crack and the juggy features around it.

Dance To It (V0) Climb the tall center face of the boulder on good jugs and sloping holds.

Terraced Garden Boulder

Dance To It

Terraced Garden

The best way to stay cool in the summer at Pine Mountain is to send your projects. Kip Gerenda ticks another one off, Painted Carnival (V3).

Painted Carnival Boulder

Painted Carnival Boulder

Finding the boulder: Follow the main trail along the right fork from the parking area, pass the No Picnic Boulder on your left, and stay right at the next fork in the trail to arrive at the base of this boulder.

Painted Carnival (V3) A classic for the area. Start under the overhang on good holds, make a move out left to a sloper on the lip, then go for the amazing pinch under the roof with your right hand and pop to the slopers out right. From here commit to the heel hook and work your way up a few more slopers and a mantle to the top.

Blunted (V3) Start just to the left of the cave at Painted Carnival. Begin with your left hand on a good edge and your right on a small knob, and make a big move to the sloping dish and mantle.

The Choadler Boulder

Finding the boulder: Just around the left corner from Painted Carnival is this lichen-covered face hiding in the shadows.

The Choadler (V4) Start on the left side of the wall with some sidepulls for the left hand and a mixture of jugs and edges for the right. Make a huge move up and right to a mini crack hold, then use slopers to work your way to the summit.

The Choadler Boulder

The Choadler

Bumfight Boulder

Finding the boulder: Just past the Terraced Garden Boulder, this is the tallest freestanding boulder on the top of the ridge—you can't miss it.

Bumfight (V0) Climb the highball arête on the southeast corner of the boulder. Lots of fun jugs and arête holds to the top.

Bumfight Boulder

Bumfight

Morally Impaired Boulder

Finding the boulder: From Bumfight, walk directly west to find this wall down a level in a pit.

Morally Impaired (V3) Another gem hiding in the shadows. There are a few variations on this problem: The classic starts on the left side on an edge and a sidepull. Make a long move up to the crimp rail and another long move to a cool lip crimp, and gun for the top from here.

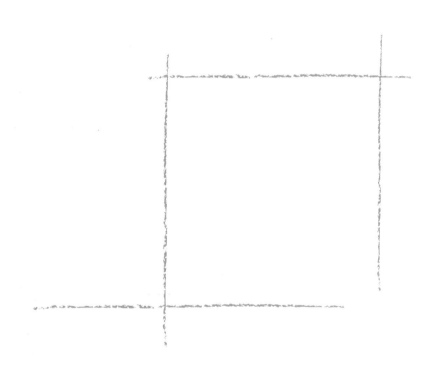

Morally Impaired Boulder

Morally
Impaired

Pine Mountain Main Area

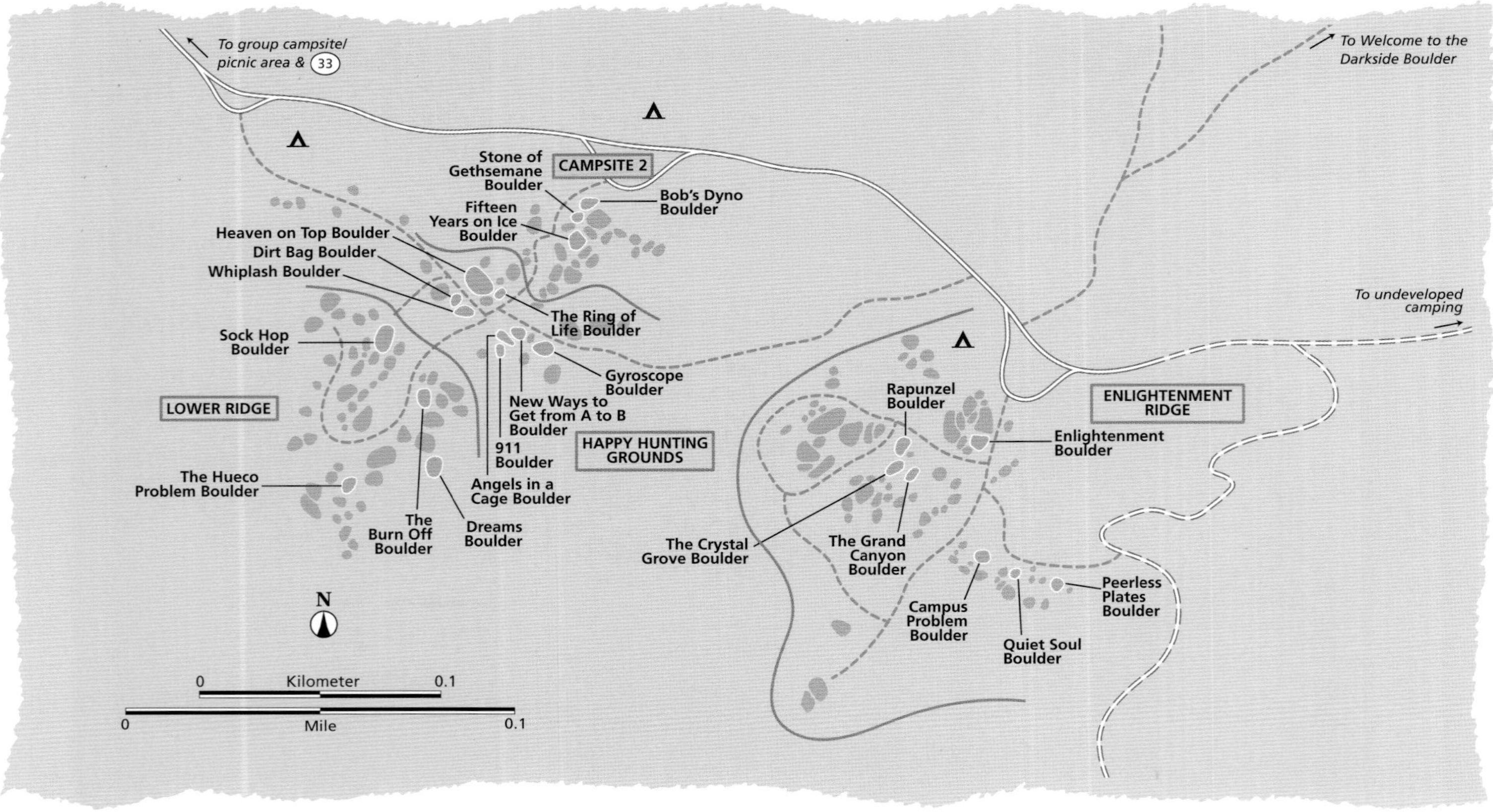

To Welcome to the Darkside Boulder

To undeveloped camping

ENLIGHTENMENT RIDGE

Enlightenment Boulder

Peerless Plates Boulder

Quiet Soul Boulder

Rapunzel Boulder

Campus Problem Boulder

The Grand Canyon Boulder

The Crystal Grove Boulder

HAPPY HUNTING GROUNDS

Bob's Dyno Boulder

CAMPSITE 2

Stone of Gethsemane Boulder

Fifteen Years on Ice Boulder

The Ring of Life Boulder

Gyroscope Boulder

New Ways to Get from A to B Boulder

911 Boulder

Angels in a Cage Boulder

Dreams Boulder

To group campsite/ picnic area & 33

Heaven on Top Boulder

Dirt Bag Boulder

Whiplash Boulder

Sock Hop Boulder

The Burn Off Boulder

LOWER RIDGE

The Hueco Problem Boulder

N

Kilometer   0   0.1

Mile   0   0.1

CAMPSITE 2

Finding the boulders: From the first group campsite, drive up the winding road past six more small campsites for 1.1 miles to a larger site with boulders in it; the main boulder here is Bob's Dyno Boulder. Please park in a pullout along the road, respect any campers, and refrain from climbing directly in the campsite if it is occupied.

Bob's Dyno Boulder

Finding the boulder: This boulder is right in the campsite.

Third Time Around (V4) Start on the left side of the wall, on the blasted-out section of rock, and climb through the short lip and to the slab on top; you can exit left for an easier variation.

Pump Action (V4) Right up the middle of the boulder is a magnetic seam that seems to draw everyone in for a go, but it's a lot harder than it looks. Sidepull your way up to the seam and get precise with your feet.

Bob's Dyno (V6) On the far right of the wall. You can start either by jumping to the sloping rail (V6), or by using some old bullet holes to climb statically to the rail; from here dyno to the top.

Bob's Dyno Boulder

Stone of Gethsemane Boulder

Finding the boulder: Around the left corner of Bob's Dyno Boulder hides a nice little warm-up, Happy Camper (V1). To access the other two routes, walk around the right side from Bob's Dyno.

Happy Camper (V1) Start sitting or standing and climb up the awesome features to a sloping topout.

Happy Camper

Happy Camper

Stone of Scone (V2) Start on the left side of the face and climb up into the arête on pinches, slopers, and edges.

Stone of Gethsemane (V2) A real gem with some stellar rock quality. Start on the right side of the face, fight the barn door, and use precision footwork as you pinch your way up the sloping arête.

Stone of Gethsemane Boulder

Stone of Scone

Stone of Gethsemane

Fifteen Years on Ice Boulder

Finding the boulder: Just at your back from Stone of Gethsemane.

Fifteen Years on Ice (V0) A wicked fun warm-up. Start on a big sloping flake and climb up this stellar face on an endless line of jugs and good edges.

Fifteen Years on Ice Boulder

Fifteen Years on Ice

Legendary climbing filmmaker Paul Dusatko puts the camera aside and shows the SoulCal crew how it's done on Dissing Euro's (V6).

The Ring of Life Boulder

Ring of Life

HAPPY HUNTING GROUNDS

Finding the boulders: From the previous group of boulders, continue walking south downhill for a couple hundred feet to The Ring of Life Boulder; right around the corner from this boulder is the Heaven on Top Boulder.

The Ring of Life Boulder

Finding the boulder: As you walk downhill on the climber's trail, you will weave through some logs and small rocks; the first major boulder you come upon is The Ring of Life Boulder.

The Ring of Life (V1) Climb the right side of the face next to the arête; use a series of small pockets and good feet to get to edges and a sloping topout.

New Ways To Get From A to B Boulder and Angels in a Cage Boulder

New Ways to Get from A to B Boulder

Finding the boulder: As you walk into the clearing from the climber's trail, this is one of the first boulders you will see in front of you to the south.

New Ways to Get from A to B (V2) Start on some small edges to climb to the sloping rail, then stem your way up the scoop using sweet slopers along the way.

Angels in a Cage Boulder

Finding the boulder: This is just west of the New Ways Boulder; you can also climb the easy crack between the two boulders.

Elysian Fields (V2) Start just to the right of the crack and climb the delicate slab with an undercling and sloping edges.

Skydiver (V5) The center of the face. Start with some tiny sloping edges and climb past a thin slot on your way to small divots, more edges, and a thank-god plate on top.

Angels in a Cage (V2) The right arête on the boulder. This is a great test of core and balance, as the climb will continually try to barn door you off. Use proper opposition and good footwork to climb this little gem.

Gyroscope Boulder

Gyroscope

Gyroscope Boulder

Finding the boulder: Walk to the east from the previous boulders; this is the rounded boulder you come across.

Gyroscope (V8) If you are looking to put your shoulder strength to the test, then step right up and throw down on this little beast. Start with a high left hand on the edge of the shotgun hole and a good edge for the foot, and make a leap to the high right sloper, then finish with a crazy high foot and one heck of a mantle.

911 Boulder

911 Boulder

Finding the boulder: Walk around to the west of the Angels in a Cage Boulder to this boulder right behind it.

911 (V8) Start with the seam on the left and a good hold around the right corner. Make a giant move with the right hand up to a sharp edge, then move left to the big sloping edge and mantle.

Heaven on Top Boulder

Frenchman's Worst Nightmare

Dissing Euro's

Heaven on Top (aka Happy Hunting Grounds)

Heaven on Top Boulder

Finding the boulder: Just past The Ring of Life Boulder is a clearing with many boulders; this one is the largest immediately to your right (west).

Dissing Euro's (V6) One of the best at the grade. Sit-start at the arête on small edges, make two hard moves, and then move up to the huge right-facing flake. Continue up and left, as the holds get bigger and farther apart.

Frenchman's Worst Nightmare (V8) On the far left side of the boulder just left of the arête. Start on two gastons and make some moves on small edges to get to the jug near the top of Dissing Euro's; finish up that route.

Heaven on Top (aka Happy Hunting Grounds) (V3) Definitely a problem on everyone's moderate highball lists, but please be careful, as this mega classic has seen its fair share of twisted ankles from a botched topout. Start standing in the middle of the main face and use a ladder of excellent edges that get bigger the higher you go. Top out to the left on some less than positive holds.

Whiplash Boulder

Whiplash

Whiplash Boulder

Finding the boulder: When you arrive in the main clearing from the climber's trail, this boulder is just to the west. There are climbs all the way around the boulder.

Whiplash (V11) This may be the first V11 a lot of climbers touch—and possibly by accident because it just looks so good and doable! There are only a few holds on the gorgeous wall and pretty much only one way to climb it. Try hard.

Surrounded By Fish

Surrounded
by Fish

Surrounded by Fish (V5) A super fun climb for the grade. Start low on the arête with good holds and work your way up past a small pocket around the left corner and to the tricky mantle on top.

Paul Dusatko sending the rig on Surrounded by Fish (V5)

Dirt Bag Boulder

Dirt Bag

Dirt Bag Boulder

Finding the boulder: This is the small boulder right next to the Whiplash Boulder.

Dirt Bag (V3) Climb up the short, blunt arête on sweet holds to the thank-god jug on top—laps are a must!

Sock Hop Boulder

Sock Hop

LOWER RIDGE

Finding the boulders: From the Surrounded by Fish route on Whiplash Boulder, walk south for a couple hundred feet to the next group of boulders.

Sock Hop Boulder

Finding the boulder: From the Surrounded by Fish route, walk southwest; you will come upon this boulder from the backside.

Sock Hop (V6) A must-do on the Pine Mountain circuit. Start on a couple of left-facing edges or a side-pull out right and make a long move up to the sloping ledge, then figure out how to top this puppy out with a mixture of bad feet, small edges, and shallow dishes.

The Burn Off Boulder

The Mantelland Hueco Problem

The Burn Off Boulder

Finding the boulder: Walk directly south from the Surrounded by Fish route to a narrow wash; this boulder is on your left.

The Mantelland Hueco Problem

(V2) Lots of fun for being a foot off the ground. Start sitting in the lowest hueco and pop up to the next huge hueco; the climbing is much easier from here.

The Burn Off (V4) Just around the corner from The Mantelland Hueco Problem. Start sitting with a good left edge and a small crimp for the right hand. Find a good heel hook and bust up right to the slopers at the lip, then work your way to the top.

The Burn Off Boulder

The Burn Off

Dreams Boulder

Dreams Boulder

Finding the boulder: Continue walking south from the Burn Off Boulder. After passing between two large boulders, turn east to find this boulder.

Dreams (V8) Start deep in the cave on a big, flat jug. Make big moves right, along the seam, and throw to a slot in the next seam; from here move up into the jugs above.

Wet Dreams (V4) From the far right side of the cave, start on edges and make a move out to the big sloping arête. Keep bumping up the arête until you can mantle up onto the face.

Involuntary Luge (V10) Chris Lindner first put up this direct exit for Dreams late in the summer of 2005—the name comes from a classic Seinfeld joke. Begin in the heart of the cave on the large, flat jug and make a few powerful moves to exit the cave directly to the jugs above.

Tuck and Roll (V10) A long traverse of the whole cave. Start at the jug in the heart of the cave, climb all the way right to the start of Wet Dreams, and finish that route to the top.

The Hueco Problem Boulder
Finding the boulder: Instead of heading east for the Dreams Boulder, continue walking south from the Burn Off Boulder. You will approach this boulder from the backside.

SoCal native Chris Lindner adds a new testpiece to Pine Mountain, Involuntary Luge (V10).

The Hueco Problem Boulder

Hueco Problem

Hueco Problem (V3) A real treasure for the area with a stellar view a few steps away. Start matched in the lowest hueco and work your way to a decent edge up and right; another hueco and a sloping arête lead to the top.

Enlightenment Boulder

ENLIGHTENMENT RIDGE

Finding the boulders: From Campsite 2, continue for another 0.1 mile down the road to another large campground with boulders in it on your right. Please park in pullouts on the road if the campground is occupied. Walk south around the main large boulder in the site; Enlightenment Boulder is immediately on your right.

Enlightenment Boulder

Finding the boulder: As you walk south from the camping area, look for the tall boulder and this climb on your right.

Enlightenment (V5 R) This climb will fry your nerves but keep you coming back for more. Start at a rock-filled pocket and work your way up to the obvious pink pebble in the middle of the wall. Stand up on it and keep moving up on more pebbles and shallow pockets.

Campus Problem Boulder

Campus Problem Boulder

Finding the boulder: Walking south past Enlightenment, you will come across a faint climber's trail on your left (east); turn here, and the Campus Problem Boulder is on your right.

Campus Problem (V4) Start sitting on a good jug. Climb through another good hold and a sloping ledge on your way to the giant hueco, then finish up on easy terrain.

Campus Direct (V6) Start sitting on the good jug, then move to a thin seam straight up the middle of the face. Crank off this to better edges at the top, avoiding the hueco out right.

Quiet Soul Boulder

Finding the boulder: Continue down the faint trail past the Campus Problem Boulder to the next major boulder in front of you.

Quiet Soul (V2) Start this lichen-speckled face on two sweet gastons and crank up on some sloping crimps to the jug in the middle of the face; big holds on the left edge lead to the top.

Welcome to the Real World (V2) Climb up the chunky highball left arête—a lot of fun with a little added height.

Quiet Soul Boulder

Quiet Soul

Welcome to
the Real World

Peerless Plates Boulder

Nirvanic
Incuts

Peerless
Plates

Peerless Plates Boulder

Finding the boulder: Continue down the faint trail from the Quiet Soul Boulder to the next major boulder.

Nirvanic Incuts (V1) This little boulder is full of warm-ups all the way around. Sit-start this route on the left side of the tall face and make one hard move on your way to glorious plate pulling.

Peerless Plates (V0) More of the same as on Nirvanic Incuts. Start on the right side of the wall next to the arête and climb through juggy plates the whole way.

The Grand Canyon Boulder

Quest for
the Chalice

The Grand Canyon

The Grand Canyon Boulder

Finding the boulder: Instead of turning left at the faint climber's trail just south of the Enlightenment Boulder, turn to the right (west) to find this boulder.

Quest for the Chalice (V1) Start next to the left arête and use opposition as you climb through a slew of left-facing holds on your way to the scooped-out jug on top.

The Grand Canyon (V2) Begin with two sidepulls and crank to the plate in the middle of the face, then grab a sloping pocket on your way to the classic mantle topout.

The Crystal Grove Boulder

The Crystal Grove

The Crystal Grove Boulder

Finding the boulder: This boulder is right next to the Grand Canyon Boulder.

The Crystal Grove (V4) A wonderful Pine Mountain slope-fest. Start with a high right hand in a decent scooped dish, paste the feet, and make a big move to nab a high left hand (if you are short). Paw your way up the sloping topout.

Rapunzel Boulder

Rapunzel Boulder

Finding the boulder: It is impossible to miss this boulder as you walk into the main sector of Enlightenment Ridge; it's the tallest one around.

Clawing at the Walls (V7) Start sitting at the lowest hueco and keep your feet on while you crank up to the larger, sculpted hueco at head height. Use a small edge and an even smaller pinch to set up for the throw to the top—exciting! The stand start is a V6.

Siege Tactics (V3) If you run laps on Rapunzel, then try this puppy on for size. Start climbing into the sloping seam that leads to small edges on your way up the highball face just right of the arête.

Rapunzel (V1) One of the best on the ridge. Start at the base of the right arête and climb through great jugs and plates to a cruxy top section, just high enough to keep your attention.

Welcome to the Darkside Boulder

Welcome to the Darkside Boulder

Finding the boulder: From the campsite where Enlightenment Ridge begins, walk north across the road and onto a faint climber's trail that leads directly up the hill. At a fork in the trail, follow the right fork. You should arrive at the massive boulder within 3 to 5 minutes from leaving the road.

All Dabbed Out (V7) Around the left side of the boulder, start on the far left side of the wall on a right-facing jug, then continue up on small right-facing holds to the top—watch your back.

Body Movement (V9) Start to the right of All Dabbed Out at the end of the sloping rail on a good edge for the left hand and out right with a good sidepull. Make a huge move up to the right-facing vertical rail, match this with precise footwork, and continue past another two sets of slanting rails. Keep it together for the highball topout.

Wanderlust (V12) This is a new addition to the boulder, put up in 2014 by Sean Crozier. Start below the top of Body Movement on a big, U-shaped undercling and make two hard moves on edges up to the vertical rails; finish up Body Movement.

It's not unusual to find yourself high above the morning clouds on the ridgeline of Pine Mountain.

Welcome to the Darkside (V11) The namesake of the boulder. Start sitting at the base of the overhanging arête with a good rail for the right hand and a pinch on the arête for the left. Heel hook your way up the arête to a big crux move and a highball slab to round out the whole problem.

Hot n' Spicy (V8) Start sitting at the base of the wall on a series of jugs in the broken flakes. Move up and right for a couple moves on right-facing holds until you can reach the small edges straight up and to the left. Continue up to the sloping lip for a serious topout.

Spicy Beaver (V10) Begin the same as Hot n' Spicy and climb to the right toward a large sloping shelf. From here continue straight up the slab above.

Beaver (V3) Stand-start at the large sloping ledge in the middle of Spicy Beaver and climb into the highball slab directly above.

Points of Interest and History

It is rumored that Yvon Chouinard and his pals on more than one occasion would come up to Pine Mountain to explore and practice for the big walls of Yosemite, the Canadian Rockies, and Patagonia, where he would later go on to put up many groundbreaking first ascents.

According to the Los Padres Forest Service, the Jacinto Reyes Scenic Byway is a 38-mile segment of CA 33 (Maricopa Highway) that passes through some of the most picturesque and diverse terrain in SoCal. The highway is the connector for commerce and tourism between the San Joaquin Valley and Southern California. Although today it is a popular scenic drive, the route maintains its feeling of solitude and isolation.

Welcome to the Darkside Boulder

Hot n' Spicy

Beaver

Welcome
to the Darkside

Spicy
Beaver

Santa Barbara Foothills Overview

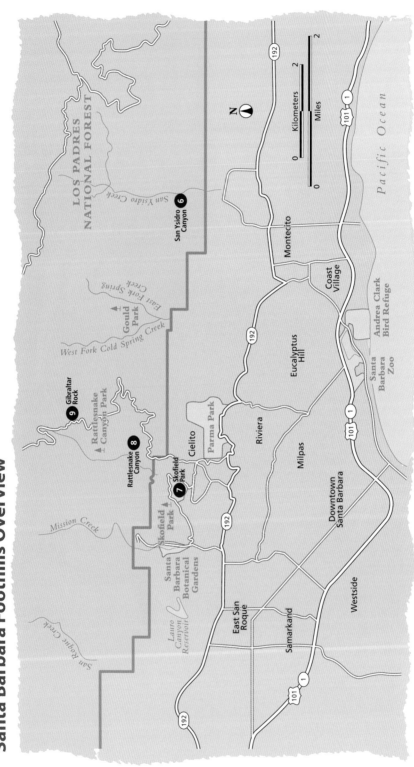

Santa Barbara County: Foothills

The lower foothills of the Santa Ynez Mountain range roll casually down to the Pacific Ocean and are dotted with some amazing sandstone climbing. The rock in the lower hills of this area is composed mostly of Coldwater Sandstone, a mixture of arkosic sandstone, siltstone, and shale, which makes this type of rock very resistant to erosion. The rock is so good in some areas that it has been compared to Fontainebleau, the fabled climbing area in France. Up along the cliffs at Gibraltar Rock, the rock changes to Matilija Sandstone, similar to what's found at Sespe and Wheeler Gorges. This rock is composed of feldspar, quartz, shale, and siltstone, which gives it a much harder and grittier feel with lots of cracks and pockets.

Climbing in the foothills is often found in rural areas including Skofield Park and San Ysidro Canyon, just on the outskirts of some of the wealthiest neighborhoods in the country, such as Montecito, Cielito, and Samarkand. However, this doesn't take away from how good the rock climbing is in this small region.

Food and drink are at their best in this region. If you are into good coffee, be sure to check out Handlebar Coffee Roasters or the Santa Barbara Roasting Company; both are just off State Street in Downtown Santa Barbara and offer delicious treats and strong coffee in a relaxing environment.

For some real authentic Mexican tacos, look no further than Lilly's Tacos, tucked away where State Street meets US 101 on Chapala Street—you won't regret the trip for these warm soft-shell tacos. If you are in the mood for a little more upscale Mexican experience, check out Los Agaves's two locations, on North Milpas or State Street, for big portions and excellent ingredients.

For those looking to keep the meal on the lighter side, check out Santa Barbara's own small business success story, The Natural Cafe. They have two locations, on State Street or Hitchcock Way, and offer a menu full of light fare including vegetarian and vegan options along with locally sourced meats and fresh-caught fish.

If you are interested in some of the culture and history woven into Santa Barbara, be sure to stop by the Old Mission Santa Barbara for a guided or self-guided tour of the church and grounds. Founded by Padre Fermín Lasuén in 1786, the mission served as a religious conversion center for the Barbareño tribe of the Chumash Native Americans. The current structures and church were completed in 1820 and now serve as a place of worship, a retreat, and a museum of the Chumash Indians. The mission is on Laguna Street; call (805) 682-4713 for more information.

Camping options for this region are far and few between. You can reserve sites at El Capitan, Refugio, and Gaviota State Parks, along the Pacific Ocean north of Santa Barbara off US 101. They are all wonderful beach campgrounds, but they fill up quickly; visit www.parks.ca.gov for more information. You can find hotels in town as well; any hotel booking site works well. It is also possible to camp at Cachuma Lake over the San Marcos Pass on CA 154. There are single sites, group sites, cabins, and yurts for reserve; find more information at www.cosb.countyofsb.org.

A local longboarder and his chase vehicle spook a gray squirrel on Gibraltar Road.

6.

San Ysidro Canyon

San Ysidro Canyon is found in a small town called Montecito, home to some of the most expensive real estate in the country. From where you park your car, you will hike past a boutique hotel and a 5-star restaurant on your way to the shady canyon of San Ysidro. Once you approach the cliff and cross the year-round stream, you are welcomed with a stunning variety of routes for all abilities on perfect Coldwater Sandstone. Temperatures can be quite pleasurable year-round due to the shade this particular canyon gets.

The climbing history at San Ysidro can be traced back to about 1975, with Rick Mosher spearheading the majority of the ascents with his team of Joe Roland, Chuck Fitch, Curt Dixon, John Chavez, and Mike Forkash. This small crew put up super classics such as Face Lift (5.7 R), Peels of Laughter (5.7 R), Many Happy Returns (5.9+), Orangahang (5.7), and Rick's Route (5.8 R), with development continuing well into the 1980s and early 1990s. The first ascensionists led these routes ground up with bold protection, and their mark can still be seen in the

Santa Barbara staple Pat Shourds takes a solo stroll up Face Lift (5.7 R) in 2006.
PHOTO MATTHEW FIENUP

San Ysidro Canyon

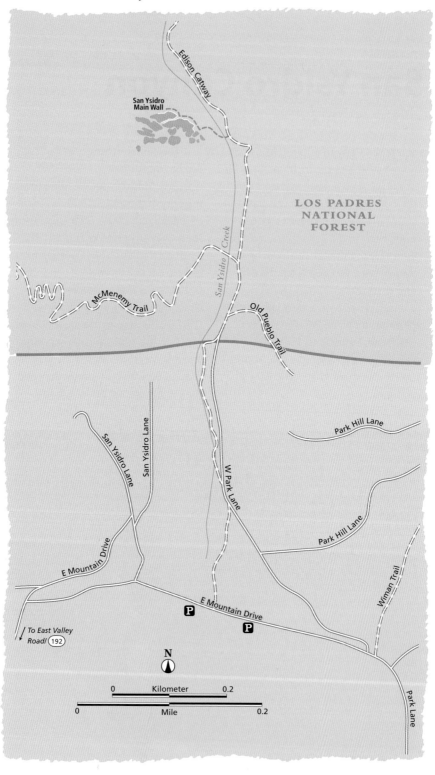

Edison Catway

San Ysidro
Main Wall

San Ysidro Creek

LOS PADRES
NATIONAL
FOREST

McMenemy Trail

Old Pueblo Trail

Park Hill Lane

San Ysidro Lane

San Ysidro Lane

W Park Lane

Park Hill Lane

Wiman Trail

E Mountain Drive

E Mountain Drive

To East Valley
Road/ 192

Park Lane

N

| 0 | Kilometer | 0.2 |
| 0 | Mile | 0.2 |

climbing and bolting style found here at San Ysidro; be prepared to run a few bolts and placements out.

Getting there: From US 101 North or South to exit 93 in Montecito, take San Ysidro Road 1 mile north toward the mountains, to East Valley Road (CA 192). Turn right and follow this for 0.9 mile, then take a left onto Park Lane. Follow this for 0.4 mile and then bear left at the fork onto East Mountain Drive; park off the side of the road here. This is a suburban neighborhood, so be sure to keep the noise down and the road clean.

Finding the crag: From the parking area look for a walking trail on the north side of the road; head north as it follows a creek bed beside a private road with homes. The trail weaves on and off the road, getting wider at times for horse travel and then shrinking back to a walking path. Continue following the trail for about a quarter mile to a gate and onto a more established walking trail in the canyon. The San Ysidro rock formation will appear on your left. Keep your eyes peeled for a large slab that angles up the hill on your right. Just past this slab is a small climber's trail on the left leading down to the creek and past a boulder; you should see a large wall across the creek at this point. Once you cross the creek, you will be at the far end of the crag.

Main Wall

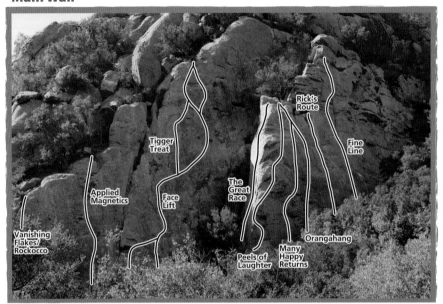

Vanishing
Flakes/
Rockocco

Applied
Magnetics

Tigger
Treat

Face
Lift

The
Great
Race

Rick's
Route

Fine
Line

Peels of
Laughter

Many
Happy
Returns

Orangahang

MAIN WALL

The main wall at San Ysidro Canyon hosts some of the finest routes in the lower foothills of Santa Barbara County. The Coldwater Sandstone is kinder to the fingers than most other sandstones found in the region, and the crag stays shady for most of the day due to the narrow canyon it rests in. These routes can be long and at times runout. To access the top of the wall, you can scramble up the 4th-class gully in the middle of the crag.

Finding the crag: Once you see the first large wall across the creek, continue down the climber's trail a little farther to find a creek crossing that will take you to the far edge of the crag near Vanishing Flakes.

Vanishing Flakes (5.11a) This burly route starts at the far left end of the main formation. The crux comes right off the bat on the first few moves up to the horizontal seam where you can clip a historic fixed pin. Continue by climbing to the right with engaging moves up to the first bolt at 20 feet, where the climbing gets a little easier. There is a thin seam just past the second bolt that takes small protection like a 1-inch cam. The crack widens as you approach the top where it joins up with Rockocco. Standard rack for the crack. 80 feet, 2 bolts to 2 bolt anchors with chains.

Vanishing Flakes

Rockocco (5.5) The easiest route on the wall and the best spot for beginners. Start just to the right of the tree and climb up the right-facing flake on jugs. After about 20 feet of climbing, you will be able to make a long traverse to the left on a slabby ledge. At the end of the ledge is the crack at the top of Vanishing Flakes that leads to the top anchors. Standard rack. 80 feet, 2 bolt anchors with chains.

Applied Magnetics (5.8+ PG13) One of the classic lines in the area. Start just 5 feet to the right of Rockocco on a thin crack with pockets in it; the protection is sparse and runout in spots as you continue climbing past the crack to a thin seam on the upper face. A single bolt protects a crux up high. This is a very serious traditional lead. Standard to thin rack. 80 feet, 1 bolt to a 3-bolt anchor.

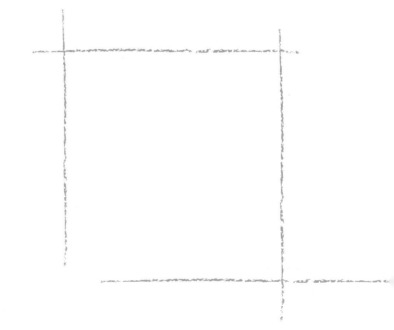

Face Lift (5.7 R) Face Lift is one of the most popular routes at the crag and can have a queue of climbers waiting their turn, but it's well worth the wait. Start just to the left of the main descent gully on either a crack or the easier flakes on the right side—multiple variations exist along this route. Bolts are placed just close enough, but you may want to supplement your rack with some midsize gear. After clipping the third bolt with a long sling, you must traverse to the right to gain the fourth bolt. From the fourth bolt you can either continue up and to the right to access a 3-bolt anchor above a large hueco, or you can climb straight up and to the left to access a 5.8 variation (Tigger Treat) with two bolts that joins back up with the main route before the top. From the 3-bolt anchor on the main route, climb up on the right-facing flakes and follow the left or right variation for the last couple bolts—climbing right toward the large hueco is 5.9; staying to the left is 5.7. Standard rack. 90 feet, 6 bolts to a pine tree and cracks for an anchor on top.

Face Lift

The Great Race (5.10a) To access the base of this route, you must scramble up the main gully to the right of Face Lift for 30 feet to a ledge where your belayer can build an anchor at the tree if need be. Climb up the face toward the first bolt to clip it; climbing in a semicircle to the left and back around to the right past the first bolt will pass difficulties to access the second bolt. From there continue up four more bolts on the face to the anchors. 70 feet, 6 bolts to a 2-bolt anchor with rings.

The Great Race

An unknown climber topropes
The Great Race (5.10a).
PHOTO MATTHEW FIENUP

Peels of Laughter (5.7 R) Chuck Fitch first climbed this route in 1975 as a free solo; it has since become one of the more popular easy toprope routes at the crag, though it is still a bold lead. Start at the base of a large apron of slab running down from the main arête. Climb up through easy friction moves toward a large corner system and traverse left at the corner to a bolt around the corner; from here you can place some gear in a crack that you must follow up and to the right back onto the main face where you can clip the second and last bolt at a shallow ledge. Traverse to the right a little and continue up to the large overhang; it's easy climbing after that to the anchors. Standard rack. 110 feet, 2 bolts to a 2-bolt anchor. If you plan on setting up a toprope, use slings to extend the anchor. **Descent:** Scramble down the 3rd-class gully or rappel The Great Race.

Peels of Laughter

Many Happy Returns (5.9+) A popular route starting just to the right of Peels of Laughter. Begin on a very thin slab leading up to a bolt and a good ledge; an easier variation is to climb up to the right on positive holds to the first bolt. Continue up the steep face past another bolt to a crack inside a left-facing dihedral. Beyond the crack a seam is the last crux you must stem your way past before easy climbing to the summit. Standard rack. 80 feet, 2 bolts to a 2-bolt shared anchor with chains; a tree is also used to rappel from.

Orangahang (5.7) Just to the right of Many Happy Returns, there is a water groove that runs right down the slab. Climb up through the groove using a 3-inch cam to protect the moves to the first bolt at a slight overhang with a slot—getting past this is the crux. Easier climbing exists above, following a low-angle thin crack you can protect with medium Stoppers or cams. Pass one more bolt, then scramble to the anchors. Standard rack. 80 feet, 2 bolts to a 2-bolt shared anchor with chains; a tree is also used to rappel from.

Orangahang Area

Rick's Route (5.8 R) The next route to the right is about 30 feet up the hill from Orangahang. Start just under a left-facing corner with a small bush, climb up through here, and clip the first bolt. From here you will encounter the crux; traverse left and make a bouldery move around the bulge to gain a small ledge and the wide crack. Continue up the crack, placing gear if necessary, to one more bolt at the end. From the bolt follow the line of huecos and sloping holds to the large oak tree at the summit. Standard rack to 3 inches. 80 feet, 2 bolts to a tree anchor.

Fine Line (5.9) This route is 12 feet to the right of Rick's Route. Begin by climbing up toward two holes. The large, shallow hueco on the left has a bolt; follow the thin seam up and to the right from here. Find another bolt above the crack that leads to easier terrain and one more bolt before you move to another crack. Follow the crack to the last bolt and the summit. Small to standard rack. 105 feet, 3 bolts to 2 bolt anchors with chains.
Descent: Rappel down right of the route to a ledge above and to the right of the base—it's a rope stretcher, so tie a knot.

> **Points of Interest and History**
> A young Yvon Chouinard visited the canyon one day in the 1970s with Sir Christian Bonnington, a world-famous alpinist from the UK who was "knighted" in 1996 for his service to the sport. At the end of Yvon and Christian's quick session, they had made the first ascent of the hugely popular Applied Magnetics (5.8+ PG13).

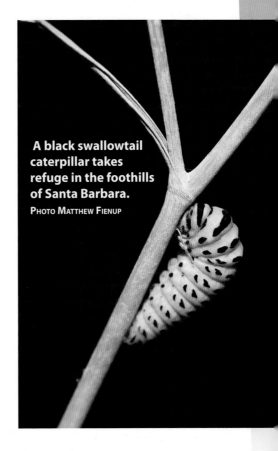

 A black swallowtail caterpillar takes refuge in the foothills of Santa Barbara.
Photo Matthew Fienup

Never a bad moment down by the stream. Mike Colee takes a lap on Bullet the Chisel Profits, the sit start to Le Fissure King (V3).

PHOTO JASON HOUSTON

7.

Skofield Park

As you wind your way up into the foothills above Santa Barbara just off CA 192, you will see plenty of state and city parks. One of those in particular offers something for climbers, Skofield Park. The locals know this little crag as "Little Bleu" for its uncanny similarity to the rock quality found in the famed bouldering area Fontainebleau in France. There is about a day's worth of boulder problems here that may possibly have you coming back to top out that one last project. The routes are scattered along a paved hiking trail and meadow in the park. One of the better boulders in the region (the Cracked Boulder) is found just next to the creek, down a small gully, offering off-the-beaten-path seclusion.

The climbing history of Skofield Park started in the late 1980s to early 1990s with two local hard men: Doug Hsu and Chuck Fitch likely established the moderate gems, little was recorded, and this area fell into the shadows of the climbing community. However, in the mid-1990s Steve Edwards, Jason Houston, Viju Mathieu, Rick Freidland, Russell Erickson, and a core group of climbers from the Patagonia shop put Skofield on the map. The only issue was that there were not more boulders of this high-quality stone! Development continues these days, albeit at a much slower pace. Recently Thomas Townsend added a new V10 named Verisimilitude to the Cracked Boulder. Although there is only a small amount of major boulders at Skofield, there are plenty of variations and hidden problems to keep your skin shredded for just one more session.

Only the best routes have been included in this book, so take some time to explore the creek. The park hours are 8 a.m. to 5 p.m. in the fall and winter, 8 p.m. to 7 p.m. in the spring and summer; the park is closed Tuesday and Wednesday.

Getting there: From US 101 North take exit 95 for Salinas Street. Follow Salinas Street for 0.9 mile to a traffic circle and take the second exit onto Sycamore Canyon Road (CA 144). Follow this for 1.1 miles and keep left at the bend onto Stanwood Drive (CA 192). Continue for another 1.1 miles and take a right onto Cielito Road. Follow this for 0.9 mile and turn right onto Las Canoas Road. The entrance to Skofield Park will be on your left after 0.4 mile. Park here in the dirt lot.

Finding the boulders: From the parking area follow the paved

Skofield Park

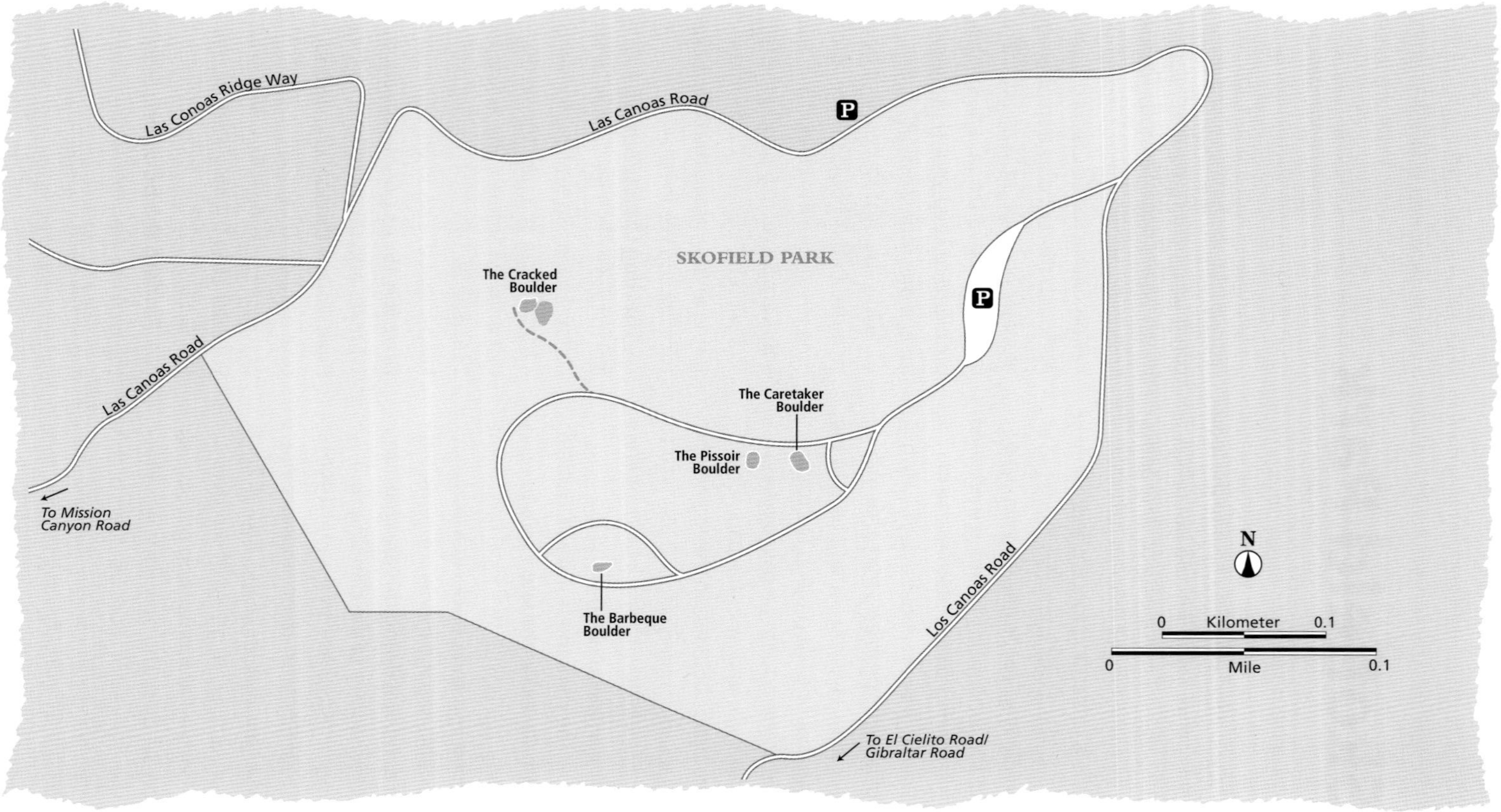

SKOFIELD PARK

The Cracked Boulder

The Caretaker Boulder

The Pissoir Boulder

The Barbeque Boulder

Las Canoas Road

Las Canoas Road

Los Canoas Road

Las Canoas Road

Las Canoas Ridge Way

To El Cielito Road/
Gibraltar Road

To Mission
Canyon Road

N

Kilometer
0   0.1

Mile
0   0.1

The Caretaker Boulder

path into the main part of the park, after a few minutes you will see the first main boulder on your right, The Caretaker Boulder.

THE CARETAKER BOULDER

A great boulder with some short moderates and a couple good high-balls rests on the side of the path. This boulder gets good shade from trees and is easy to scramble off. You will surely be the center of attention to the other park visitors while climbing on this boulder.

Finding the boulder: The Care-taker Boulder is the first you come to as you enter the park; it is just off the left side of the paved loop if you take the right fork once you enter the park.

Zerreissen (V4) Start down in the pit on a curved, sloping ramp and make some slopey moves straight up to top out. A spotter eases the mind with the rocks at the base of the climb.

Igemma (V3) Sit-start on the small rock with your hands on the large ledge, make some moves left, and then climb up on tricky slopers.

Undercarriage (V4) Sit-start on top of the flat boulder to the right of the main cave, climb up and to the right on fun holds, and continue by topping out using some crimps. For a longer climb begin deep down in the main cave and climb out the ribs.

Undertaker (V6 R) Start in the back of the main cave and climb directly out the ribs and up the face. Be sure to have good spotters and pads for the highball crux over the bad landing.

To a Grave (V5 R) The left side of the main cave. Start on a left-hand jug on the outside of the cave and climb up to the sloping ledge, then make a committing move up high to top out. Starting in the cave bumps the grade to V6/7, depending on height.

The Caretaker Boulder

The Pissoir Boulder

THE PISSOIR BOULDER

This little boulder sits just off the path under some trees for shade. There are some excellent sloper problems here on the main vertical face. You can easily scramble off the backside.

Finding the boulder: From the Caretaker Boulder continue down the paved path for another minute until you see this boulder on the left side under a clump of trees next to a service hut.

Piss-Off (V1) Start on a left-handed sidepull on the left side of the face, establish on bad feet, and make the big move to the slopers and top out.

Bodily Functions (V2) Straight up the center of the face through a bulge; use high sloping edges to gain the top slopers.

2 Francs to Glory (V4) Climb the blunt arête on the right side of the face. Start with slopers and establish on the arête to gain the upper edges and slopers. Use the boulder at the base to make it a V1.

The Pissoir Boulder

Fert Loaf

Bobie (V6) Jump-start to two wide pinches and wrestle your way to the top on more slopers. Start on the boulder at the base to make it a V1.

Fert Loaf (V0) Short but fun. Sit-start as low as you can on the left-leaning ledge, then bust moves up and left to gain the top.

The Barbeque Boulder

Chunks O' Flesh

Gorehound

Roco

THE BARBECUE BOULDER

If you have some burgers and sausage to cook up, then head over to this boulder. Not only are there great little warm-ups all around this standalone block, but there is also a barbeque right next to it ready for some grilling. You can easily scramble down the boulder.

Finding the boulder: When you first enter the park, head onto the left side of the paved walking path and follow this to where the path splits; in between the split is the boulder.

Chunks O' Flesh (V1) On the left side of the face near the barbecue grill. Start on two good edges and climb up to another good left-hand edge, then make a big move to the top slopers.

Gorehound (V0) Start the same as Chunks O' Flesh but with your right hand on a sidepull; head slightly to the right and up from here.

Roco (V0) The fun arête with great moves on the right-hand side of the face.

The Cracked Boulder

THE CRACKED BOULDER

Arguably the best and hardest boulder in the park, and quite possibly the best setting in the park as well (make sure not to leave any trash down here by the creek bed). The Cracked Boulder has been climbed on for years, and yet new lines still go up to this day, like the most recent V10 addition in 2013 by Thomas Townsend, Verisimilitude. You can easily scramble off the backside of the boulder.

Finding the boulder: From the main path, walk past the Pissoir Boulder, continue for another minute, and look for a small hiking path on your right heading down toward the creek. This path leads past a small picnic area and to the creek bed. You will come up on the backside of the Cracked Boulder; walk around to the left or scramble down over the right side.

Bullet the Baby Blue Sky (V2) The sweet-looking arête on the left side of the face is a lot trickier than it looks. Start with a really high sidepull; a cheat stone or stacked pads may be necessary for shorter climbers.

Verisimilitude (V10) This recent addition to the park is the sit start to Bullet the Baby Blue Sky. Begin on the huge sloper at the bottom of the arête, get a heel hook on the right, and figure out how to top it out. A fantastic line for the grade and very temperature dependent.

The owner of Vesper Vineyards in San Diego, Chris Broomell, squeezes the juice out of the edges on Mutants Amok (V5).

PHOTO SEAN NAUGLE

Le Fissure King (V0) The crack in the boulder. Start standing and make a couple moves on fun edges to the top. For full value sit-start and make a painful finger lock to gain the upper portion of the crack; this variation goes at V3 and is known as Bullet the Chisel Profits.

She Made Me Do It (V8) A wonderful traverse that starts on the far left side of the boulder, with the left hand on the far left sloper and the right near the start for Le Fissure King. Make some long moves as you work your way right, toward the start of Mutants Amok, finishing on that problem.

Points of Interest and History
Skofield Park was once owned by Ray Skofield, one of the original founders of Los Rancheros Vistadores, an elite men's horse riding club, who eventually donated the land to the city.

Mutants Amok (V5) The mega classic of the park. Start on a good hold under the overhang, bust a huge move up to the lip, and balance your way to the top.

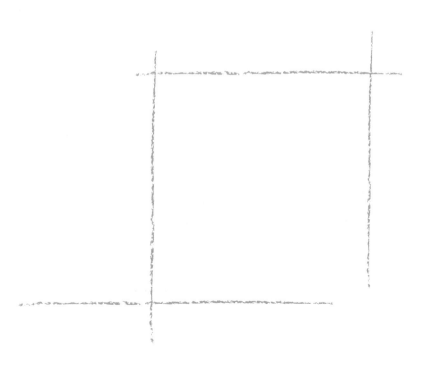

Rattlesnake Canyon

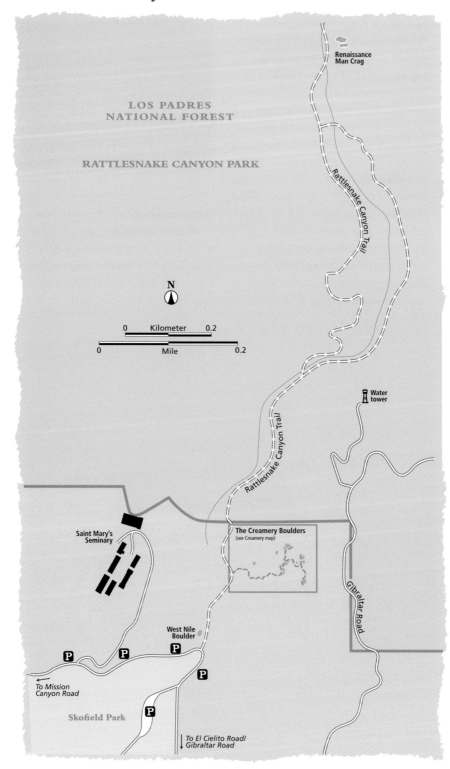

8.

Rattlesnake Canyon

Just up the canyon a short ways from Skofield Park is a popular hiking trail through Rattlesnake Canyon, and no, there aren't rattlesnakes there. However, typically there is running water in Rattlesnake Creek at some point on the trail even during the hottest of summers.

Rattlesnake Canyon consists of three main areas with a mix of bouldering and sport climbing along the trail. The history of the area is very spotty at best. It is thought that most of the rock here had been seen for years, with the earliest climbing

potential possibly being discovered in the 1970s by Amos Clifford. The first major recorded development in the area though was when Mike Forkash and Gary Anderson put up two classics at the top of the canyon on the Alchemist Wall in 1980 (not in this guide). The region subsided into the shadows of obscurity for many years until most recently when a flurry of development helped put the entire canyon back on the map. Down in the base of the canyon in 2008, Galen MacDougall and friends "rediscovered" the Creamery Boulders after

On a gorgeous autumn afternoon, local blacksmith Andy Patterson runs a cooldown lap on West Nile (V3).

the Tea Fire ripped through the hillside revealing the area to the world again. Early in 2013 Matthew Fienup and Andy Patterson helped add new routes at the Alchemist Wall and the Renaissance Man Crag, respectively. There can be poison oak along the trail or near the rocks so always keep an eye out for where you are walking.

Getting there: From US 101 North take exit 95 for Salinas Street. Follow Salinas Street for 0.9 mile to a traffic circle, take the second exit onto Sycamore Canyon Road (CA 144). Follow this for 1.1 miles and keep left at the bend onto Stanwood Drive (CA 192). Continue for another 1.1 miles and take a right onto Cielito Road. Follow this for 0.9 mile and turn right onto Las Canoas Road. After 0.4 mile drive past the entrance to Skofield Park on your left; continue for another 0.1 mile to where the road takes a left turn at a stone bridge; this is Rattlesnake Canyon. Park at any of the dirt pullouts along the sides of the road.

Finding the boulders: From the parking areas walk back to the stone bridge; the West Nile Boulder is accessed by following a path from the west side of the bridge, and the other areas are accessed by following a hiking trail on the bridge's east side.

WEST NILE BOULDER

Locals have seen this boulder for years, but it seems that until recently it hadn't seen much attention besides the warm-up route. In 2013 Andy Patterson and Thomas Townsend scrubbed the moss off the harder lines and added some new ascents to the block. After finishing a good bouldering circuit at Skofield Park, this is a great boulder to walk up the road to and get on some harder lines. The setting is very peaceful in the creek bed, which depending on the year and season can be dry or running. Lots of trees provide bits of shade throughout the day.

Finding the boulder: From the main pullouts on Las Canoas Road, walk to the stone bridge and follow the path that leads up canyon on the west side of the bridge. Within a couple hundred feet you will see the boulder on your left.

West Nile (V3) This was the original line on the boulder; it's now the warm-up for the harder lines to the right. Start on the big jug down low and make a big move up to the scoops, then move to the left to top out.

West Nile Boulder

Le Bernd (V5) Begin this problem just to the right of the previous route on the small prow. Start sitting with a sloper for the left hand and a decent edge for the right, make a cruxy move with the left hand up to an edge, and dial in some fancy footwork to go straight up from here.

Le Privett (V7) A couple feet to the right of Le Bernd is another hard sit start. Begin with the left hand on a decent edge, right hand on a smaller crimp, and make a big move right to a large sloper sidepull and eventually into an undercling. With some footwork and hand switches, make your way to the jug up and right. Very beta intensive.

Skin O' My Teeth (V9) A nice long traverse for the grade. Start on West Nile and work your way right, all the way to the start of Le Privett. Finish up that problem.

Countdown to Extinction (V10) This problem was put up by Thomas Townsend in the winter of 2013 and is a crowd favorite for the grade. Begin on Le Privett and make a cruxy move to the left to get onto Le Bernd and finish up that route.

The Creamery

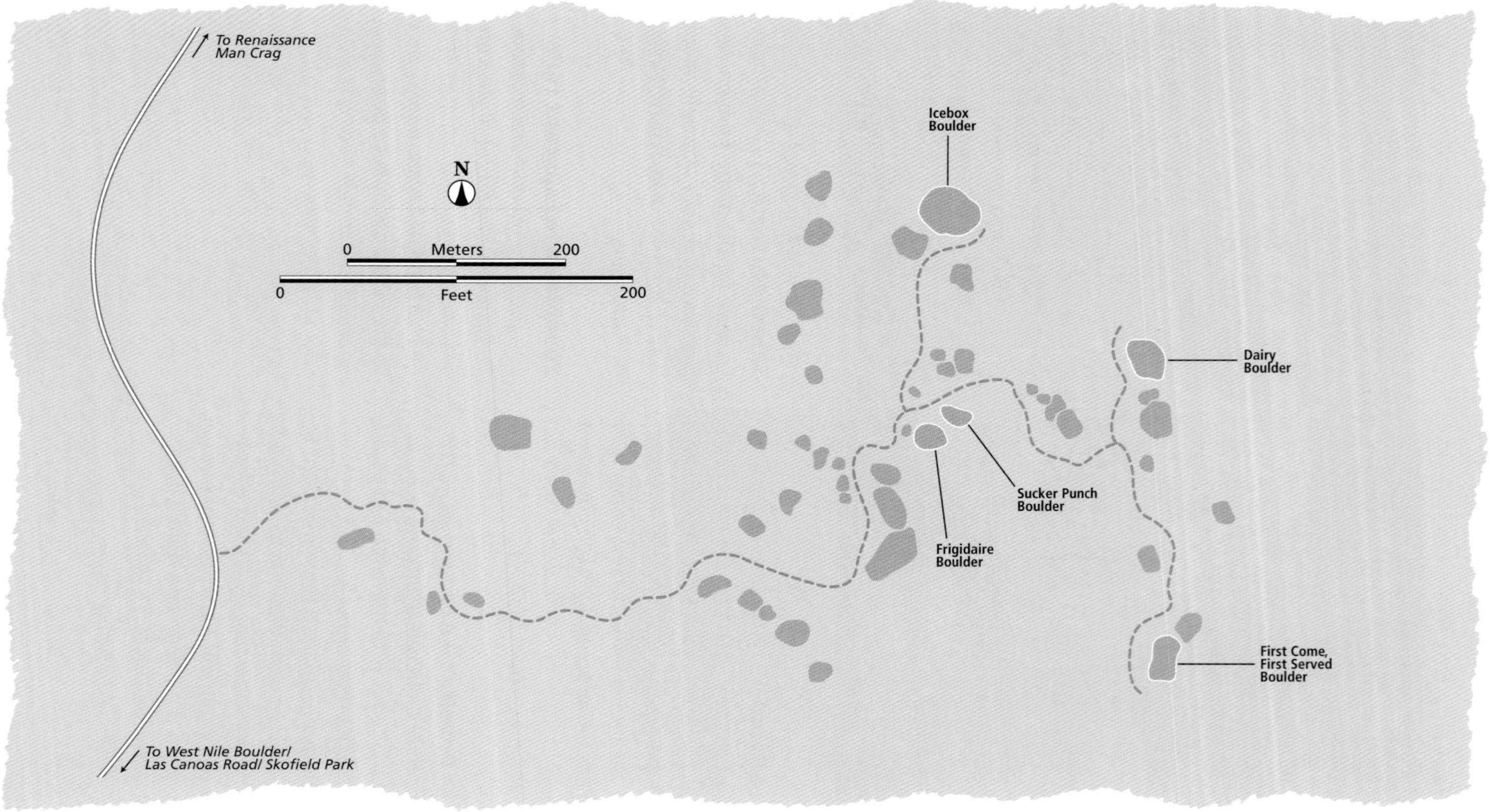

To Renaissance
Man Crag

N

Meters
0   200

Feet
0   200

Icebox
Boulder

Dairy
Boulder

Sucker Punch
Boulder

Frigidaire
Boulder

First Come,
First Served
Boulder

To West Nile Boulder/
Las Canoas Road/ Skofield Park

THE CREAMERY

The Creamery was likely first discovered in the 1970s when Amos Clifford was on one of his rock hunting missions, but it wasn't truly developed until the great Tea Fire of 2008 that opened the boulders back up to the public eye. Thomas Townsend and Kelly Lindsay spent some time on the hillside to scope out the boulders, but in the summer of 2013 Andy Patterson spent a good deal of time making a legitimate trail to each little sector and building proper landings at a couple of the boulders. Now this area hosts a handful of amazing problems with some of the toughest sandstone around—it can sometimes resemble granite.

Finding the boulders: From the main pullouts on Las Canoas Road, walk back to the stone bridge and hike up the trail on its east side, following along the creek as you hike up the canyon. After only 0.1 mile you will see a nice climber's trail on the right that leads directly to the Creamery Boulders and right to the base of the Frigidaire Boulder. Reference the map to locate the other boulders, which are all within close proximity of each other.

Andy Patterson stays cool on the crux topout of Frigidaire (V6/7).

Frigidaire Boulder

Frigidaire

Buckets
Forever

Cookies
and
Crimps

Frigidaire Boulder

Finding the boulder: This is the first major boulder you will come to as you follow the main climber's trail up the hill.

Buckets Forever (V2) The boulder's plumb line and a great warm-up for the rest of the boulder field. Jump-start to the hueco and work your way up and slightly right following the line of good holds.

Frigidaire (V6/7) Right in the middle of the tall face lies a deceptive little line. Start with the right hand on a weird edge and the left on a small sidepull, bust a move to a small pocket with the right, and then climb into the left-leaning rail. Climb straight up through hidden edges to the top.

Cookies and Crimps (V4) Around the corner from Frigidaire, start in a pocket for the right hand and a good edge for the left, then climb up through sloping edges to a great slab topout.

Sucker Punch Boulder

Finding the boulder: This boulder sits just to the north of the Frigidaire Boulder.

Sucker Punch (V5) This short little route packs a punch. Sit-start on the left-facing edge and make a move up to the right to a good edge, then reset the feet and bump up to the lip to top out.

Fast and the Flurrious (V7) Very tricky route that can be done many ways. Sit-start with the left hand on a small crimp and the right on a small sidepull, make a big move out left to a sloper, and bump your right hand up the bulge.

Sucker Punch Boulder

Icebox Boulder

Icebox Boulder

Finding the boulder: Follow the climber's trail and keep to the left at the Frigidaire Boulder to walk right up to this boulder.

Icebox Slab (V0) Not on topo. The far left side of the Icebox Boulder. Climb up the slab with the hole in the middle of it.

General Electric (V5) Start on the large jug at the base and a heel hook out left, then make a long move to the sloping rail. Continue up and to the right on edges and slopers.

General Steampunk (V6) A slightly harder variation to General Electric. Start the same, then move to the left and up off the first sloper rail.

Dairy Boulder

Dairy Boulder

Finding the boulder: From the Sucker Punch Boulder, continue walking on the climber's trail uphill to a junction where you can turn north or south; walk north to find this boulder.

Lactose Tolerant (V4) Start with a high edge (some climbers may have to stack a pad to reach it), get established on the slab, and follow the right-facing flake up the wall.

First Come, First Served Boulder

First Come, First Served Boulder

Finding the boulder: At the trail junction at the top of the hill from the Sucker Punch Boulder, turn right and walk south to this boulder.

First Come, First Served (V10 R) The V10 gem of the area. Sit-start in the back of the cave and make a powerful move to gain the sloper pinch on the exit of the cave. Match the crimp rail and continue up the highball face.

For an easier variation, start on the left-hand edge of the cave on a short arête and move to the large sloper pinch (V7). Very temperature dependent; bring lots of pads.

Pop, Lock and Drop (V6) On the far right side of the wall. Sit-start on some slopey rails, work your way up to the next major ledge, and dyno to the top.

RENAISSANCE MAN CRAG

This small trailside area has seen recent development, with the newest hard line put up in March 2013 by Andy Patterson. There were already signs of climbing, and Mike Forkash and Gary Anderson are presumed to have put up the original bolts and anchors at the crag, but little is known about the detailed history of the older routes. The small cliff sees a good amount of shade and has a couple of great moderates as well. This is a popular hiking trail, so you are likely to see a lot of day hikers coming up and down the canyon.

Finding the crag: From the main pullouts on Las Canoas Road, walk back to the stone bridge and follow the trail on its east side. Hike this trail past the side trail to the Creamery Boulders and continue for a total of about 1.2 miles, or about 30 minutes of hiking up the canyon. You will know you have arrived when you drop down toward the creek in a very shady area of the canyon. The main walls are up on your right from the trail.

Sword in the Stone (5.10a) The excellent climbing on great rock is worth the hike up the canyon. This route never has a line at the base and is full of fun movement. This may have been one of the original routes climbed at the crag—old bolts were found when recent development began in 2011—but it's well protected now. Start on the left side of the slab and climb up past a series of horizontal cracks, patina edges, and slopers to the top. 8 bolts to a 2-bolt anchor.

Elijah Ball on Trebuchet (5.13a) at Renaissance Man Crag, Rattlesnake Canyon
PHOTO BERND ZEUGSWETTER

Sword in
the Stone

The Wicked Dude
Takes a Wife

The Wicked Dude Takes a Wife (5.8)
A fun traditional route. There are quite
a few ways to top the route out, but
the easiest way to top out for a rappel
is described here. Start to the right
of Sword in the Stone and climb up a
bulge onto the main slab. Use a series
of disappearing cracks and ledges
to climb up and eventually to the
left toward a final hand crack to the
right of Sword in the Stone's anchors.
80 feet. **Rack:** Standard rack up to 2
inches, long slings. **Descent:** Rappel
off Sword's anchors. This route can
also be used to access the top of the
other wall for toprope setup.

Points of Interest and History
Always on the hunt, Amos Clifford was known to explore
the steep hillsides and deep
canyons of Santa Barbara for
rocks and wild herbs; it is quite
possible he was the first to
walk into what is now known
as the Creamery Boulders. The
area was originally dubbed Zen
Grids and Squares, and has also
been referred to as the Scorpion
Boulders.

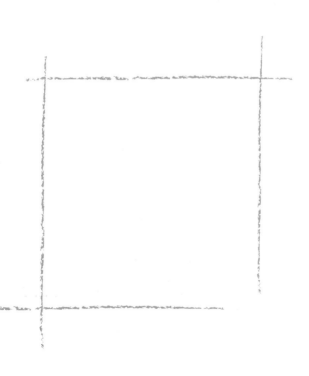

The Black Death (5.12c) Start on the far left side of the wall on a large jug on the ledge, move up to the huge undercling, and make a series of hard bumps with the left hand up past the feature. A couple more moves get you right beneath the huge suspended boulder and then to a thank-god jug on the corner for the right hand. 3 bolts to a 2-bolt anchor.

Bring Out Your Dead (5.10a/b PG13) In the middle of the wall, start on some chunky holds and work your way into the broken bottom section of a crack. Climb up the finger crack to a good stance where you can get your first piece in. Continue along the crack to a mantle, then move straight up a short face on good holds past a bolt to a 2-bolt anchor. **Rack:** Small rack in the .05-inch range, one quickdraw, slings.

Trebuchet (5.13a) This route and the next are the two most recent additions from Andy Patterson, put up in 2011 and 2013, respectively. Start at the arête where your belayer can clip in for safety. Begin with a pinch for the left hand and an undercling pocket for the right, then set up for a dyno to the jug on the arête with the right hand. Make some tricky moves to get into the flared crack on the right; follow this to the last bolt and a jug. Make one last huge move to an edge that leads to easier climbing to the top of the crag. 4 bolts to a 2-bolt anchor.

Renaissance Man (5.13b/c) This is the right-hand start to Trebuchet. Begin under the overhang below a beefy bolt on an undercling, and climb through some burly movements on bad edges and pinches to access the flared crack above, where the route joins the end of Trebuchet. 4 bolts to a 2-bolt anchor.

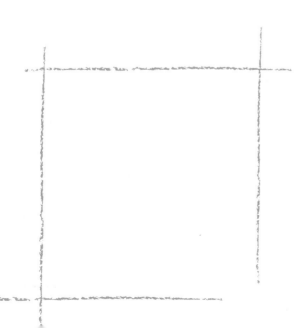

Gibraltar Rock

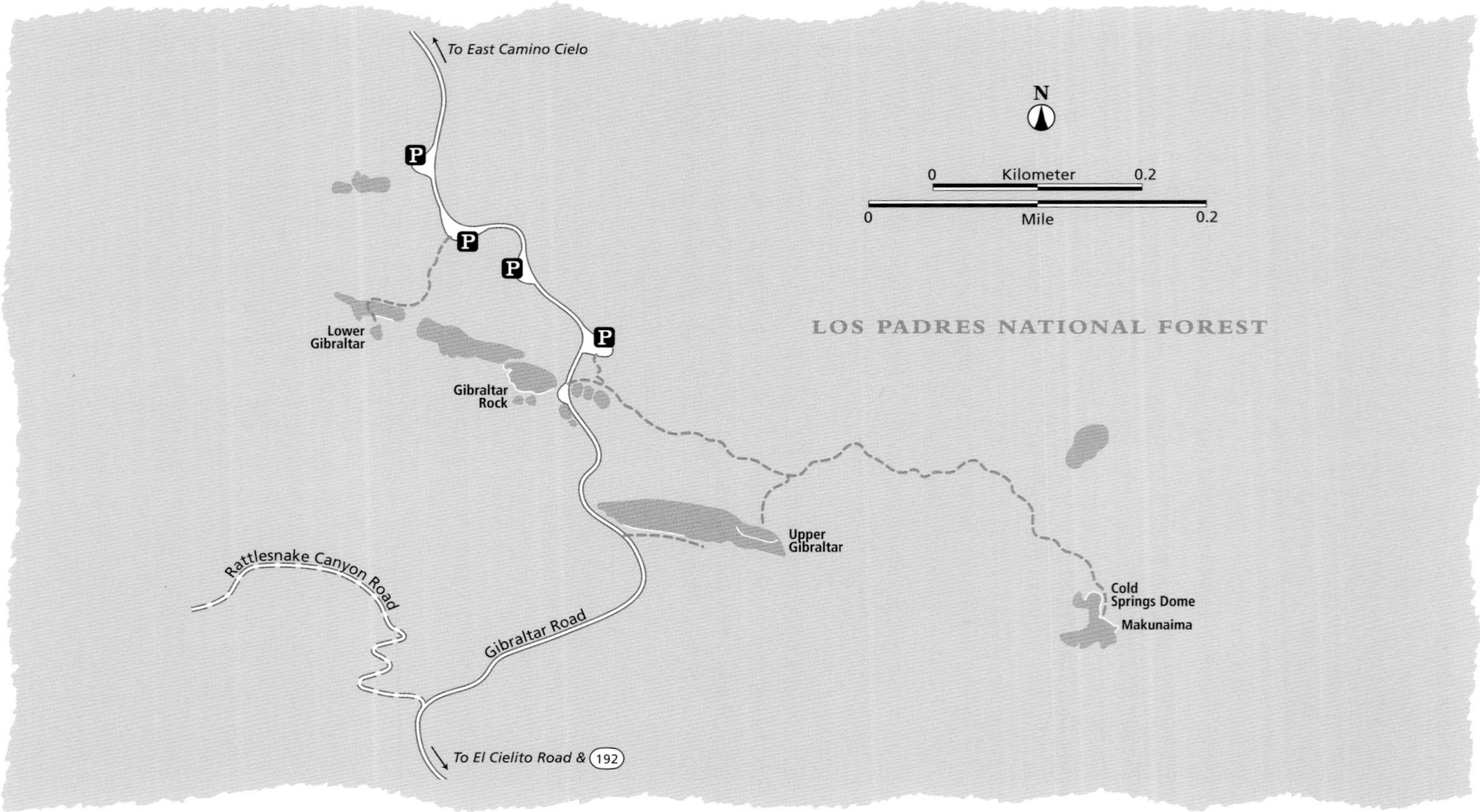

LOS PADRES NATIONAL FOREST

To East Camino Cielo

Lower Gibraltar

Gibraltar Rock

Upper Gibraltar

Cold Springs Dome

Makunaima

Gibraltar Road

Rattlesnake Canyon Road

To El Cielito Road & 192

N

Kilometer

Mile

0   0.2

0   0.2

9.

Gibraltar Rock

Gibraltar Rock is the oldest and most popular place to climb in Santa Barbara County if you want to lead climb or toprope. High above the city, the main formations offer views that can't be beat. Oftentimes you can spot eagles, falcons, and the occasional hang glider floating in the thermal vents high above the cliffs. With the majority of the climbing available only a few feet from the road, Gibraltar can get crowded on the weekends. It's not uncommon to find the local colleges' climbing clubs setting up numerous topropes on Lower Gibraltar's South Face. The Gibraltar area hosts multiple crags, all with their own feel, so if one crag is crowded you can just hike a few minutes and usually find a whole wall to yourself. Note that the road is used by many bicyclists, longboarders, and motorcyclists, so be aware of who is on the road when crossing to get from cliff to cliff. Most of the cliffs face to the south and can be extremely hot during the summer.

The history of Gibraltar Rock can be traced all the way back to 1954 when Herbert Rickert put up some of the very first routes on the main Gibraltar formation, such as The Ladder (5.5). Herb was responsible for the outstanding classic T-Crack (now a 5.10b lead), which he put up in 1956 with direct aid. Using the same techniques, Herb also ascended The Nose (now a 5.11a lead) in 1960. Development continued through the 1960s with many ascents going unrecorded. It wasn't until the 1970s that people started to take notice of the area when Gibraltar started seeing some action from the likes of Amos Clifford, Chuck Fitch, Steve Fitch, Joe Roland, Kevin Brown, Jeff Smith, and Jim Donini. When Cold Springs Dome was discovered, a new flurry of first ascents occurred, starting with Rick Mosher aiding up the now classic Makunaima (5.11b). In the mid-1970s the legendary Henry Barber free climbed the first on-sight ascent of Euell Gibbon (aka The Nose), and this continued the trend to free climb many of the routes that were originally aided. In the 1980s Cold Springs Dome and Upper Gibraltar saw multiple new lines go up with the help of big wall superstar and speed climber Hans Florine. During this time Hans helped to establish more of the old aid lines as free routes. Gibraltar seemed to have been "all tapped out" for a few years. Maybe, however, the crag just needed a fresh set of eyes.

In 2010 locals Bernd Zeugswetter and Andy Patterson began adding a string of techy 5.12s on the West Face. Who knows what the future will bring to this historic climbing area.

Getting there: From US 101 North take exit 95 for Salinas Street. Follow Salinas Street for 0.9 mile to a traffic circle and take the second exit onto Sycamore Canyon Road (CA 144). Follow this for 1.1 miles and keep left at the bend onto Stanwood Drive (CA 192). Continue for another 1.1 miles and take a right onto Cielito Road. Follow this for 0.5 mile and turn right onto Gibraltar Road (FR 5N40). Continue on this windy road for 4.4 miles until you see the main formation of Gibraltar Rock on your left. There are many dirt pullouts along the sides of the road and a larger parking area on the right just past the main Gibraltar formation.

Finding the crags: From the main parking area, you can access all the main crags. For directions to each crag, see the specific descriptions.

A rare look into Santa Barbara's climbing past—Herbert Rickert works for the first direct aid ascent of T-Crack (5.10b) in 1956.
PHOTO DAVE ARMSTRONG

GIBRALTAR ROCK SOUTH FACE

Undoubtedly the most popular cliff in all of Santa Barbara, the South Face is where groups gather to learn climbing skills, where beginners jaunt up their first lead, and where tourists come to check out the views from the easily accessible summit. Here is where Herbert Rickert led the crag's first route, The Ladder (5.5), back in 1954; you can still follow his historic footsteps up this perfectly situated route. Most the routes here top out around 100 feet, so a 70-meter rope is required for toproping and rappelling.

Finding the crag: From the main parking area or any of the pullouts on the road, walk toward the main formation; there is a small climber's access trail right next to a man-made rock wall on the road. You can either hike to the top of the wall to set up topropes, or you can access the bottom of the crag by hiking down into the gully.

The Nose (5.11a) This steep crack has become one of the testpieces for anyone climbing in the area. Start under the large roof on the left-hand side of

Gibraltar Rock South Face

the South Face. Follow the steep hand crack up through the roof and over the lip to anchors where you can rappel. **Rack:** Standard rack of cams from 1 to 3.5 inches. It is possible to extend the route to the top of Gibraltar Rock by ascending easy but questionable 5.6 terrain to the summit anchors; from here you can walk off or make a long rappel off chain anchors.

Smooth Arête (5.12c TR) Scott Cosgrove first climbed this often forgotten route in 1986. Climb the nearly blank arête just to the left of The Nose. The climbing is very exposed, and large swings are common, so set up a toprope from the anchors at the end of The Nose crack.

Klingon (5.9 R) A great route up the middle of the South Face of Gibraltar Rock. Start just to the right of The Nose and follow a dihedral up toward a ledge where you will climb toward a left-facing corner. Climb up the corner and follow it out to the left using underclings and face holds to another ledge. From the ledge continue up the face to the top. A bolt and some gear can be used on the top for an anchor; there is also a boulder that can be slung. **Rack:** Standard rack up to 4 inches.

Mid-Face (5.6 R) A great beginner route for toproping in the middle of Gibraltar Rock. Start just to the left of The Ladder, or start the same as The Ladder—many variations exist. Climb up to the first main ledge, then move up and left to the summit of the face. As a lead it can be a bit runout. An anchor can be set with two bolts on the summit. **Rack:** Standard rack up to 3 inches.

The Ladder (5.5) Herb Rickert first ascended this route in 1954; it was the first route to be toproped and free climbed in Santa Barbara County, and it was eventually protected with fixed pitons for many years. Start the route on a face just to the right of a crack on the right side of the formation. Climb up the face and then traverse left to the main crack; follow this crack up to a major ledge. From the ledge you can climb more difficult terrain through the right side of the overhang; it is easier to traverse left or right to bypass the difficulty. Continue to the top following the rest of the crack. Build an anchor at the top or use the bolts from Mid-Face. **Rack:** Standard rack from 0.5 to 4 inches.

As the last of the sun peeks through, Becca Polglase nears the top of The Rapture (5.8).
Photo Matthew Fienup

GIBRALTAR ROCK WEST FACE

The West Face of Gibraltar Rock hosts some of the most New Age, hair-raising, hard face climbing around, along with one of the most popular 5.10s in the county, T-Crack. This face features one of the more beautiful sandstone shapes you may ever see: The huge ripples in the middle of the face are called conchoidal fracture planes, where a large chunk of rock has fallen off and you can see how water affected the outcome of these particular sedimentary layers of Matilija Sandstone.

Finding the crag: From the main parking area or any of the pull-outs along the road, walk toward the main formation to find a small climber's access trail. You can hike up to the summit to set up topropes or hike down into the gully to the base of the South Face and follow this around to the bottom of the West Face and the Sea of Holes and Northwest Corner routes.

T-Crack (5.10b) This is the most bomber crack you will find in the county—the sandstone here is as good as it gets, and the views are just as good. To access the start of this route, you must either hike over and around Gibraltar Rock to the Peanut Gallery Ledge, or you can take the less direct route and climb the easy Northwest Corner. Good hand jams lead to a tricky mantle with protection at your feet. You can build your own anchor at the summit or use existing bolts 25 feet over the lip (be sure to have a long sling). **Rack:** Standard rack from 0.5 to 2 inches.

Self Reflection (5.11b/c) An oldie but a goodie, first climbed in 1987 by Kevin Brown and Mitch Jan, challenges climbers with very thin and technical face climbing. There are a couple ways to access this route: You can rappel down to the three-bolt hanging belay from the summit, or you can climb the first part of T-Crack and then traverse the main ledge to the right to an alcove with a bush in the corner, climb around the bush to the three-bolt hanging belay. The first part of the route requires gear up to 4 inches; the technical upper headwall is equipped with three bolts. Bolt anchors on the summit over the lip.

Broken Mirror (5.12a R) This route was originally an aid route called Mirror in the Bathroom; it was led clean by Andy Patterson and Bernd Zeugswetter in 2011. Start from a hanging belay you rappel to from the summit. Long runouts and technical moves embody this route that leads to the summit, joining up with Self Reflection for the last few bolts. 8 bolts to a bolted anchor over the summit.

Jabberwocky (5.12a R) This variation to Broken Mirror is worth the mention, a New Age gem added in 2012 by Andy Patterson and Bernd

Gibraltar Rock West Face

Zeugswetter. Start as for Broken Mirror and clip its first two bolts, then climb through a roof to a jug and clip the bolt to the far left. This is where you climb into Jabberwocky and stray from Broken Mirror. Climb through open hand crimps, tricky footwork, and long deadpoints to access the hanging belay on Self Reflection. Finish up the last three bolts of Self Reflection. 7 bolts to bolt anchors on the summit.

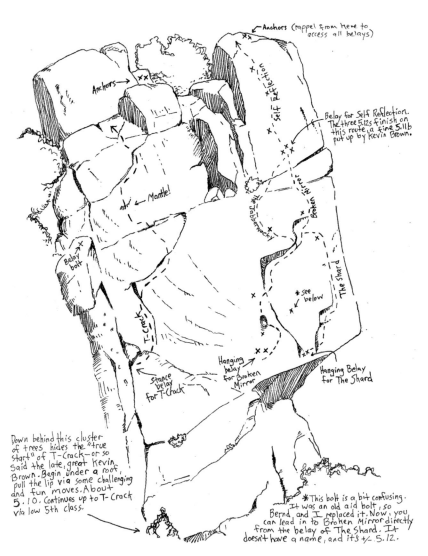

One of the wonderfully hand-drawn topos by master artist Andy Patterson; keep your eyes peeled for his upcoming book with the rest of his collection.

PHOTO ANDY PATTERSON

The Shard (5.12c R) The last addition from the Andy and Bernd team in 2013, The Shard starts from a hanging belay to the right of Broken Mirror; access the belay stance by rappelling in from the summit. The climb starts up a slabby dihedral, and after surmounting the cruxes of the dihedral you are faced with an all-out slab-dyno to the left. Gain the jug below the third bolt of Broken Mirror and continue to the summit via Broken Mirror. 7 bolts to bolt anchors on the summit.

Any Minute Now (5.6) This route has been climbed for many years now, and no one knows who was the first ascensionist. There are many small pitches to this climb that can be accessed from a variety of locations. One option is to begin from the base of the cliff just around the left corner from The Nose; from here climb up through cracks and slabs toward the Northwest Corner and the Peanut Gallery Ledge. Continue along a hand traverse to the right toward the large corner, then climb up through the chimney and crack to a bolted anchor. **Rack:** Standard double rack from 0.5 to 3 inches with long slings for the traverse.

Northwest Corner (5.1) The easiest way to climb to the Peanut Gallery and the start of T-Crack. Begin from the base of the West Face of Gibraltar next to a tree and climb up the main corner to the Peanut Gallery with a 2-bolt anchor. **Rack:** Standard to large rack.

Sea of Holes (5.8 TR) Just to the left of Northwest Corner (see South Face topo) is a great route full of fantastic small pockets, shallow dishes, and holes.

Hjördis Rickert climbs T-Crack (5.10b), following in her father Herb's footsteps nearly sixty years after his first ascent.
PHOTO BERND ZEUGSWETTER

Lower Gibraltar

The Rapture

Conundrum

Lieback Annie

LOWER GIBRALTAR

Lower Gibraltar is a small sector that is worth checking out for its seclusion from the main crag and its stellar corner crack, Lieback Annie (5.7).

Finding the crag: As you drive to Gibraltar Rock, continue for another 0.2 mile past the main formation to a left-hand turn in the road with a pullout on the left; park here. From the pullout a small climber's trail leads down toward the Gibraltar gully. Follow this trail for a couple of minutes as it bears to the right and follows the top of a rock formation; you will be standing on top of the routes. Continue to follow the rock formation down and around to the left as you scramble to the base of the wall.

Lieback Annie (5.7) This is a great beginner's route to crack and corner climbing, and an easy toprope to set up due to the approach. The start is a runout lead for the first 15 feet; this leads to some amazing lieback moves up the right-facing corner. 2 bolts and hangars on the top. **Rack:** Standard rack up to 4 inches.

Conundrum (5.7 TR) Start as for Lieback Annie but climb to the left of the corner on the face, which can be toproped easily by using the 2-bolt anchor. This is a very runout lead due to the lack of gear to start, but you can clip bolts on the far left if leading. Climb up thin edges and flakes to a thin seam near the top.

The Rapture (5.8) Great, very well protected climbing on the left side of the arête. Start the same as for the previous two routes but head directly to the left toward the arête. 8 bolts to a 2-bolt anchor on the summit.

UPPER GIBRALTAR

If you are looking for some great exposure high above the city limits, be sure to scramble up to this crag and hop on one of the old classics like The Crescent (5.8) or A Route Runs Through It (5.10c). You may be lucky enough to have an audience of paragliders and hang gliders.

Finding the crag: To access the upper reaches of Gibraltar, you can take one of two paths. A small climber's trail leads steeply out of the main parking area past some large boulders and up to the top of the ridgeline. From the top of the ridge, follow a faint trail across the top of the cliffs. You will eventually be above the Upper Gibraltar Cliff and can set up topropes here or rappel to the lower ledge to start most of the routes listed in this guide. The other option, which requires some navigating through bushes and ledges, is to walk on the road from the main parking area to the base of the Upper Gibraltar cliff to find a 3rd-class approach to the routes; this path will likely have more poison oak in the spring and summer months. The routes are long here, so be very aware when lowering and rappelling, and be sure to have a 70-meter rope. On many routes it is best to walk off.

Triple Overhang (5.6) This is the first route you will encounter when approaching from the roadside cliffs, and is the leftmost route on the wall. Climb up a wide crack on lower-angled terrain to a large ledge where you climb to the right past some vegetation to the next wide crack system. Continue up past more bushes to an overhang near the summit. Follow the final crack to the top. You can also split this route into two pitches because it is about 130 feet long. A rack with some extra-wide gear is recommended.

Dazed and Confused (5.10b) This route is the first line of bolts from the left side of the wall just past a small gully. Climb up the thin face past the first set of bolts to a nice ledge where you can set up a belay (though this is not necessary as the route can be led with a 70-meter rope). If you are stretching this into one pitch, you can place gear at the ledge and then

Gibraltar Rock

Upper Gibraltar

continue up the thin seam before you arrive at the next set of bolts to the summit. 13 bolts and a small rack lead to bolted anchors on the summit. The route is about 120 feet, so beware when lowering your partner.

A Route Runs Through It (5.10c) Just to the right of Dazed and Confused is another well-protected sport route. Climb up the face with a tricky start past some bolts to a ledge and a steep roof. Climb past this and finish straight up the middle of the face on crimps and great face holds to the top. 13 bolts to a bolted anchor. The route is 110 feet, so make sure to bring a 70-meter rope.

The Crescent (5.8) The classic crack on the upper headwall. The Crescent starts as Triple Overhang up to a major ledge with lots of vegetation. Climb to the right to the next major wide crack and follow the left-curving crack up to where it joins with the end of A Route Runs Through It and its last few bolts to the top. The route is 120 feet, so be sure to have a 70-meter rope. **Rack:** Standard rack up to 4 inches; a few bolts can be clipped on the last part of the route. **Descent:** Walk off or make two rappels.

The Crescent Direct (5.9) The start of this route is just to the right of A Route Runs Through It. Start on a thin crack up a level from the main tier. The crux is early as you negotiate the thin crack with minimal gear until you reach the first major break in the wall. From here follow The Crescent to the summit. The route is 110 feet. **Rack:** Standard rack up to 4 inches, thin gear or nuts for the thin crack; a few bolts can be clipped on the last section of the route. **Descent:** Walk off or make two rappels.

The Soul (5.11b) The hardest route on the wall can be found just 30 feet uphill from the start of The Crescent Direct. Scramble up a loose gully to the start. Climb on the face through three bolts to a large ledge; from here continue into a bulge where you will find

the crux. Climb past more bolts up the middle of the face to the left of the crack. The route is 100 feet long with eleven bolts; bring gear for the anchor or use the bolts atop A Route Runs Through It.

The Gibbon (5.10b) This route shares the same start as The Soul, but once you get to the large ledge, head to the right toward the large crack systems. Follow the bolt line around the bulge where you make a spooky move to the next bolt—small gear will help protect a bad fall. The route continues up past seven more bolts to the summit. 100 feet. Build an anchor or use the bolted anchor on top of A Route Runs Through It.

Bernd Zeugswetter climbing Broken Mirror (5.12a), one of his and Andy Patterson's newest additions to Gibraltar
Photo Hjördis Rickert-Zeugswetter

COLD SPRINGS DOME

Cold Springs Dome was originally discovered in 1974 by Steve Tucker and Amos Clifford, and was quickly adopted as a popular crag to escape the heat; this is one of the few areas that receive a lot of shade during the day due to its orientation. Clifford and Tucker's discovery of Cold Springs Dome led to the rapid development of the Makunaima Wall, a wonderfully steep wall.

Finding the crag: A small climber's trail leads steeply out of the main parking area past some large boulders and up to the top of the ridgeline. You will eventually be above the Upper Gibraltar Cliff; continue hiking on the climber's trail, which sometimes resembles an old fire road. As the road/trail starts to descend, you should see Cold Springs Dome sticking out of the gully to the right; look for a climber's trail that leads down a steep ridgeline to the base of the crag.

Post-Modern Retro Classic (5.10b) As you hike down to Cold Springs Dome, this will be the first route you notice. Scramble to the base of the climb and make committing moves to clip the first bolt, then continue up the overhanging face to the top. 4 bolts to a 2-bolt anchor. This can be set up as a toprope by scrambling up the gully to the right.

Gypsy Moon (5.10d TR) Scramble down and left of Post-Modern Retro Classic to start Gypsy Moon, climbing the gorgeous arête. Set up a toprope by scrambling to the summit up the gully to the right of Post-Modern Retro Classic.

Master Cylinder (5.9+ R) Scramble down to the base of the large apron coming off the dome to start next to a right-facing corner. Climb up some fun blocky holds through a series of small cracks to the base of an overhang, place some gear, and lieback the left side of the overhang to the upper section of the route. Climb past three bolts on the way to the summit. 100 feet. **Rack:** Standard rack up to 3 inches; slings will be handy on this wandering route. Build an anchor on the summit.

Cold Springs Dome

Snidley's Whiplash (5.8) To access the next two routes, continue hiking down the climber's trail around the base of the dome to the slab on your right. Start this route under a large hueco and climb up the line of huecos and pockets, placing gear whenever you can find a spot, to a small roof. Climb past the roof to the first bolt and continue past two more bolts to a ledge. 80 feet long, 3 bolts to a 2-bolt anchor. **Rack:** Small rack from 1 to 3 inches is handy to get to the lone bolts on the route. You can continue past the ledge to the summit on less than desirable 5.7 terrain.

Magic Bag (5.9 R) Just to the right of Snidley's Whiplash. Climb up a long runout to the first bolt, then continue on long runouts past two more bolts to a shared anchor with Snidley's Whiplash. You can continue this route up the upper headwall on blocky ledges and ramps—it's an adventure. The first pitch is 80 feet long with three bolts and a shared 2-bolt anchor.

Bernd Zeugswetter on top of Gibraltar Rock
Photo Hjördis Rickert-Zeugswetter

MAKUNAIMA WALL

Makunaima (Mah-ku-nah-EE-mah) is the name of a South American Creator God and is also part of the Venezuelan legend that the Sun and an Indian woman from the water created the children of the world and named them the Makunaima. Aside from the legend of the name, this small cliff offers some of the steepest lines at Gibraltar Rock, and almost constant shade throughout the day. All the routes are topropes; scramble up around the left side of the wall to easily access the anchors. Makunaima (5.11b) is the only route on the wall that can be led on traditional gear.

Finding the crag: To access this hidden wall, follow the directions to Cold Springs Dome and continue to follow the climber's trail down and around the east side of the dome; you will see this overhanging wall in front of you after getting to the base.

Anasazi (5.10b TR) On the far left side of the main wall lies a short toprope route that ascends a lieback flake up to a large hueco at the top. To access the summit you can scramble up around the left side of the formation. Make sure to bring long slings or a length of rope to build an anchor; there are a couple sets of bolts on the top.

No Woman, No Cats (5.11d TR) Start just to the right of Anasazi and climb through a series of shallow dishes and tricky face moves to the top. Access the top to build an anchor the same way as Anasazi.

Triple Link-up (5.12b TR) This long toprope route will take you through a variety of routes and cruxes across the wall. Start as for No Woman, No Cats and work your way up and to the right into the crux of Homo Erectus. From here continue moving to the right into Makunaima Direct and to the top. You can scramble around the left side to access the top and the anchors to set up a toprope.

Makunaima (5.11b) The only route that can be led on the wall (though it's typically toproped). Start by climbing up large huecos on your way to a wide, leaning crack on the left, then climb up to a horn where you can catch a quick rest. From here continue past the horn into finger jams through the crack systems on your way to a small roof with huecos. Past the roof lie a few more finger jams that lead to easier climbing up and left to the top. About 90 feet, 3-bolt anchor on top. **Rack:** Double rack from 0.5 to 4 inches.

Makunaima Direct (5.11d R) Climb Makunaima up to the roof, just past this section continue climbing straight to the top through a tricky runout section. Same gear as for Makunaima to a 3-bolt anchor.

Makunaima Wall

Kneeanderthal

Makunaima
Direct

Homo
Erectus

No Woman,
No Cats

Predators Keep
the Balance

Anasazi

Triple
Link-up

Makunaima

Jericho
Dude

Homo Erectus (5.11c TR) Start as for Makunaima. When you get to the horn on the route, start climbing straight up toward the top of the wall, moving away from the crack system. You will encounter a small roof (crux) on the way to the summit. Access the top by scrambling around to the left.

Jericho Dude (5.12a TR) A few feet to the right of Makunaima is a direct start that climbs through a face of tiny edges and pockets below a huge hueco. Continue past this to the roof on Makunaima and finish that route to the top.

Kneeanderthal (5.11b TR) Start as for Makunaima. Climb to the roof section, but instead of going directly up the roof, traverse to the right toward a corner and then continue up toward a large roof, which you climb around on the left side to bolted anchors on the top.

Predators Keep the Balance (5.12b TR) Just to the right of Jericho Dude is a tricky orange and white face that leads directly to the top of the wall. Follow up through small edges and sloping pockets toward a large roof near the top, then climb through a series of pockets on the right side to a bolted anchor on top. You can also climb to the left under the roof to finish on Kneeanderthal.

Points of Interest and History

The original name for Gibraltar Road, weaving high into the mountains above Santa Barbara, was La Cumbre Trail. When the road workers encountered a huge, blocky rock formation on the hillside, they decided to name it Centinela del Abismo, or the Sentinel of the Abyss; this eventually was changed to the more common name, Gibraltar Rock.

The Nose, also known as Euell Gibbon, was first aid climbed by local legend Herbert Rickert in 1960. This prolific route was later free climbed in the early 1970s by Jim Donini or Steve Gerdson, and finally on-sighted by a visiting Henry Barber in 1974.

Santa Barbara County: Camino Cielo

Driving along the Camino Cielo is a must-do for anyone visiting Santa Barbara. This "Sky Road" transports you to another land, high above the Pacific Ocean and into the clouds, and on many days, above the clouds. It's no wonder with these views and elevation that the Camino Cielo is a draw to the majority of people coming to climb in Santa Barbara County. Lots of tourists take the drive along the crest as well as many road bicyclists, dirt bikers, and motorcyclists, so be cautious on the weekends when everyone is out. Most days in the afternoon, when the thermals start to pick up, it's not uncommon to see a handful of paragliders, hand gliders, hawks, and falcons alike taking advantage of the free energy. There are many jumping points for gliders off the Camino Cielo, so keep your eyes peeled.

The bouldering along the Camino Cielo is second to none. Between Lizard's Mouth, the Brickyard, and the Painted Caves, there is enough bouldering here to keep you busy for quite a few seasons. The Lizard's Mouth was likely the first area to be climbed in the Camino Cielo region only because it was the most obvious rock formation to put a rope on. Chances are there was "practicing" and

Maynard, the zebra, grabs some breakfast on Camino Cielo West. Maynard is a rescue who lives on a nearby ranch, so check your speed on your way to the crag!

Camino Cielo Overview

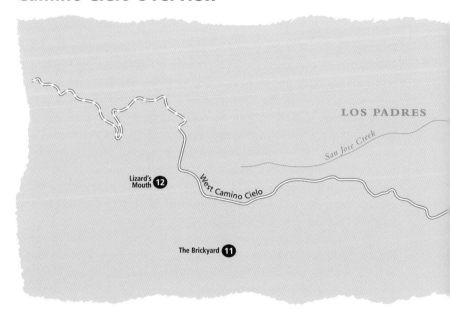

toproping at the Painted Caves years prior, but nothing was documented. Now the three major bouldering areas and their surroundings host over 400 boulder problems, and there continues to be more and more discovered hiding in the brush along the hillsides and off the sides of the road here. If you are looking to take a beginner out for an easy toprope day at a beautiful location, be sure to check out the Crag Full O' Dynamite at the opposite end of the Camino Cielo.

The rock is of the Matilija Sandstone style and can still be a little loose at times. Be sure to wait the appropriate number of days after a rainstorm before climbing at any of these locations.

After a long day of climbing out on the Camino Cielo, it's not a bad idea to head down to State Street in town and get some grub at one of the plethora of great restaurants here. If Thai is your calling, be sure to check out Zen Yai Thai Cuisine at the corner of State Street and West Haley Street; their Thai Tea is perfect to cap a long day of climbing, and their Tom Kha soup is some of the best around. Also be sure to check out El Buen Gusto, an authentic Mexican staple in

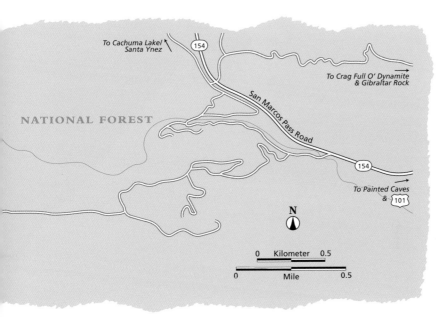

the Santa Barbara culinary lineup; they can be found on Milpas and East Canon Perdido. Be sure to taste their sauces if you are into hot, authentic spice. If you are in the mood for a quieter and cozier environment, check out the hidden Cold Springs Tavern, just over the San Marco Pass on Stagecoach Road. Grab a tri-tip sandwich on the weekends when they barbecue right outside with a live band, family style!

Camping options for this region are few and far between. You can reserve sites at El Capitan, Refugio, and Gaviota State Parks, along the Pacific Ocean north of Santa Barbara off US 101. They are all wonderful beach campgrounds, but they fill up quickly; visit www.parks.ca.gov for more information. You can find hotels in town as well; any hotel booking site works well. It is also possible to camp at Cachuma Lake over the San Marcos Pass on CA 154. There are single sites, group sites, cabins, and yurts for reserve; find more information at www.cosb.countyofsb.org.

A lone cyclist nears the end of his hill
climb up Painted Cave Road.

10.

Painted Caves

The Painted Caves are one of the more unique bouldering areas you will ever visit. If you ever played hockey or baseball in the road as a kid, you'll remember the process of spotting a car coming, all your buddies clearing the roadway of the gear while waiting for the car to pass, then yelling the standard "Game on!"

Well, imagine that while climbing a stunning highball arête—the Trojan Boulder hangs right over the road at a steep angle with the stunning Trojan Arête (V8+ R) just tempting any climber coming through this area. The Painted Caves have been a constant heartbeat of Santa Barbara bouldering. With their incredible ease

Painted Caves

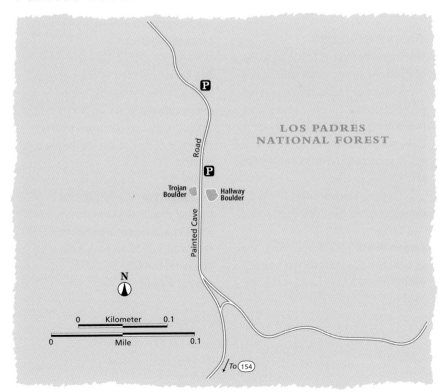

of access and variety of routes tall and short, easy and hard, it's no wonder crowds gather here on a weekly basis throughout the year. And don't forget to "Climb on!"

Getting there: From US 101 North or South, take exit 101b for State Street and CA 154/Cachuma Lake. At the end of the ramp, drive north on CA 154 for 5.5 miles into the mountains to the junction with Painted Cave Road on your right. Follow this road for 1.5 miles; you will drive right under the Trojan Boulder. Park in the dirt pullouts on the right side of the road, and be respectful because this is still a rural area.

Finding the boulders: Walk back to the boulders you just drove your car under.

TROJAN BOULDER

The Trojan Boulder is home to some of the most classic moderates at the caves. The side facing the road is full of moderate face climbs, along with the stunning masterpiece only for the bold, the Trojan Arête (V8+ R). You can easily scramble/climb down the backside of the boulder.

Finding the boulder: This is the boulder on the west side of the road.

Trojan Arête (V8+ R) A stunner, this definitely is the eye catcher of the area. There is a lone bolt on the top

to toprope this line. If you plan on bouldering, bring lots of pads and spotters. Sit-start at the base of the arête and make some crux moves to gain better holds at head height. Continue up the right side of the arête as you climb out over the road with a very highball finish into the scoop on the right.

Heavy Traffic (V3 R) This was one of the original lines climbed by Doug Hsu and Chuck Fitch in the early 1970s. Climb the direct line of pockets straight up the tall face; keep it together for the highball finish.

Big Traffic (V4) Start the same as Heavy Traffic and climb to the major hueco in the middle of the route, then move to the right and into the finish of Big Deal.

Big Deal (V6) Start to the right of Heavy Traffic on the big crimp, make a big opening move up and right to a gaston, and continue up the face. The crux comes at the last move to the top.

Old Soft Hsu (V3) Just to the right of Big Deal. Start with your left hand in an undercling and your right on a sidepull. Make long moves to edges up the face and to the hairraising topout.

Trojan Boulder

Arête of Troy (V0) Climb the left side of the arête at the far right side of the boulder.

Troy Lite (V0) Start on the arête and climb to the right side of the arête to the large holds.

Backside Traverse (V0) Not on topo. This traverse is found on the backside of the boulder away from the street. Many variations exist on the fun little traverse.

Points of Interest and History
Just up the street a little from the bouldering, the Chumash Painted Cave State Historic Park hosts a large protected site of ancient rock art. Vandalism had to be stopped, so a gate now protects the paintings inside this deep cave.

Hallway Boulder

HALLWAY BOULDER

The Hallway Boulder is a great all-around boulder. With some easy slabs, hard technical climbs, moderate overhangs, and traverse variations, it has something for everyone. Please be aware of the foliage around the base of the boulder and try not to trample anything living.

Finding the boulder: This is the boulder with the steep roof on the east side of the road.

Hallway Traverse (V0) A great traverse that is full of variations. Most start on the roadside and traverse from right to left toward and under the roof.

Street Corner (V0) A fun little warm-up on the arête next to the road.

Wedgie Roof (V6) Start under the roof on a large hueco and climb up to the roof through a line of pockets heading toward the arête. Make some painful finger locks to gain the top.

Geneva Damico warming up at the Painted Cave Boulders
Photo Sean Naugle

No Knees (V0) This climb starts under the left side of the roof. Climb through excellent edges and exit on the left side of where the roof ends. The crux is the topout.

Sloth Arête (V0 R) Around the corner from No Knees. Climb up the awesome arête just to the right of a bush and tree.

Hallway Boulder

Hallway Boulder

Sloth Arête

Baby's Head

Static Eliminator

Break on Through

Baby's Head (V1 R) This highball follows a line of good holds up to the final lunge to the Baby's Head hold; commit to the topout from here.

Static Eliminator (V4) Just to the left of Baby's Head. Stand-start on decent edges and pockets and climb up and left into a small, right-facing corner; the topout is a thrill ride. Sit-start at the large crimp rail for a V7 variation.

Break on Through (V9/10) On the far left side of the wall. Begin with two sidepulls, make a couple of hard moves to the right, and then continue up with long pulls on small holds—a very height-dependent climb.

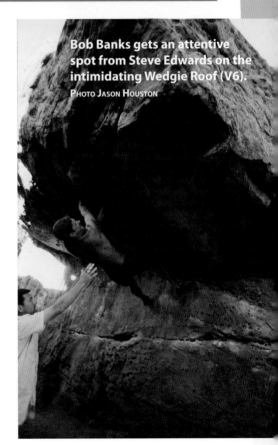

Bob Banks gets an attentive spot from Steve Edwards on the intimidating Wedgie Roof (V6).
PHOTO JASON HOUSTON

The Brickyard

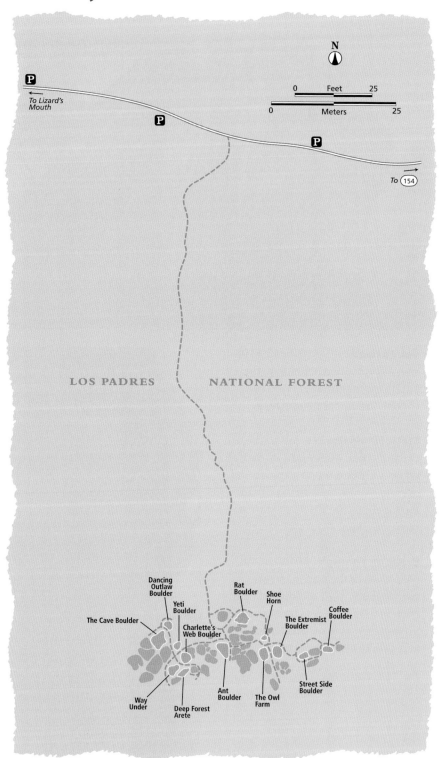

N

To Lizard's Mouth

To 154

0 Feet 25

0 Meters 25

LOS PADRES   NATIONAL FOREST

Dancing
Outlaw
Boulder

Rat
Boulder

Shoe
Horn

Yeti
Boulder

Coffee
Boulder

The Cave Boulder

The Extremist
Boulder

Charlette's
Web Boulder

Way
Under

Ant
Boulder

The Owl
Farm

Street Side
Boulder

Deep Forest
Arete

11.

The Brickyard

The Brickyard is one of those places you just wish went on forever. The climbing on the boulders hidden in this dense hillside is just incredible, although it did take a true effort from the locals to make this a destination bouldering area. At one time most of the boulders were hidden from view, covered by dense sagebrush, poison oak, and trees. It is claimed that in the 1980s Jim Tobish and John Mireles cut the first official trail down to the first cluster of boulders, and it would seem a fair assumption that they plucked the main gems at this cluster. But traction never caught on for the area, and it went into the shadows for a while. In the early 1990s a motivated

Just another beautiful spring day on the way down to the Brickyard
PHOTO SEAN NAUGLE

Marc Soltan decided it was time for a trail upgrade, so he helped widen the overgrown footpath into a good trail for climbers. Marc began cutting more trails to the outlying boulders and started putting the good word out to the locals that the Brickyard was cleaning up. Throughout the early to mid-1990s, Steve Edwards, Mike Colee, John Perlin, and Jason Huston really helped put the Brickyard on the map by bringing the total number of climbs up to one hundred, including such classics as The Extremist (V1), Grotesque Old Woman (V8), and Yeti (V4). After this resurrection of the crag, along came hyper-motivated local Bob Banks in the late 1990s. Bob was passionate about his time at the Brickyard and helped add another fifty-plus quality boulder problems by the year 2000. Bob spent days alone cleaning and working projects, giving us the mega classics The Dancing Outlaw (V8) and See Ya' at the Yard, Meat (V5). Bob released his ultimate Santa Barbara bouldering guide, *Oceans 11*, in 2003; unfortunately this guide is out of print, but it was what helped bring the Brickyard to the public eye outside of sleepy Santa Barbara.

The rock here can be friable at times; but over the course of all the years this area has been climbed, the most popular routes now feature some of the best stone around. The Brickyard is shaded by large trees and can be cooler during hot days, but this also means that when it rains it can stay wet longer. Be sure to check the weather before heading up to the Brickyard to ensure you have waited three to four days after a rainstorm to climb—the rock is porous and can break easily when wet.

Getting there: From US 101 North or South, take exit 101b for State Street and CA 154/Cachuma

Buck Branson gets gritty on Mr. Witty (V7).

Lake. At the end of the ramp, drive north on CA 154 for 7.1 miles into the mountains to the junction with West Camino Cielo Road on your left. Turn here and follow this winding road for 3.4 miles to pullouts on your right and left. There is a guardrail on the ocean side of the road with a sign that says, No Shooting Behind This Sign.

Finding the boulders: From the pullouts on the road, walk to the guardrail and look for a path in between the bushes. This opens up to a large meadow where the trail becomes obvious. Follow the trail downhill for less than 10 minutes to access the main area.

COFFEE BOULDER

This was one of the later areas to be developed at the Brickyard, but it has proved to hold some goodies, in particular Paradise Blend (V4). This small zone sees less traffic and can be quite shady.

Finding the boulder: As you hike down the trail toward the boulder field, before you arrive at the base of the Ant Boulder, look for a trail that leads off to the left. Follow this trail around the left side of the Rat Boulder. The trail weaves through some bushes and comes to the Owl Farm, passing Shoe Horn on your right. Follow the trail to the left around the side of the Extremist Boulder and to the base of its namesake route, then continue around to the left toward the tall, blunt arête of Street Side Boulder. The trail splits; follow to the right past Grin and Bear It and scramble down to ground level, or follow to the left where the trail thins out and weaves through some tall plants and back toward the Coffee Boulder.

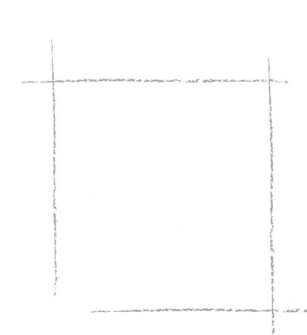

Single Shot (V2) Climb up the left side of the scooped-out red face to a pocket for the right hand; a cruxy mantle guards the top.

Paradise Blend (V4) Just around the corner from Single Shot, start on the right side of the arête on good holds and make a long move left to a sloper. Continue up to a set of slopers on a ledge and make a big move to the hueco at the top.

Coffee Boulder

Coffee Boulder

Paradise
Blend

STREET SIDE BOULDER

Finding the boulder: Follow the directions to the Coffee Boulder. The Street Side Boulder is located at the trail split just before the Coffee Boulder; the trail leads to the base of the Street Side arête.

Street Side (V0) Good fun for the grade. Climb the blunt arête with occasional pockets and lots of open-handed holds up to a committing highball finish.

Street Side Boulder

Grin and Bear It (V6) On the back-side of the boulder are two stiff face climbs. On the left side Grin and Bear It sit-starts on a crimp shaped like a smile. Make a move to a small pinch crimp and then to another small edge out right. Continue to the right to the top of South Street.

South Street (V4) Another strong face climb. Start matched in a big sloping hold and work your way straight up through sidepulls and more slopers to the top.

Street Side Boulder

Grin and Bear It

South Street

THE EXTREMIST BOULDER

Home to the extraordinary tall face called The Extremist (V1 R), this is a must-do for any highball aficionado, and a great line to add to your solo circuit if you like high blood pressure. Scramble down the side onto another small boulder.

Finding the boulder: Follow the directions to the Coffee Boulder. The base of the Extremist Boulder is just past Shoe Horn and before the Street Side Boulder.

The Extremist (V1 R) Follow a series of pockets, scoops, and edges up the tallest section of the wall, fully engaging all the way to the last move over the lip.

Moderate (V1 R) Start just to the right of The Extremist on a pair of pockets, then move up and to the right on good edges and gastons. Lots of balance is necessary to top this line out.

The Extremist Boulder

The Extremist   Moderate

THE OWL FARM

Finding the boulders: As you hike down the trail toward the main boulder field, before you arrive at the base of the Ant Boulder, look for a trail that leads off to the left. Follow this trail around the left side of the Rat Boulder. The trail weaves through some bushes and comes to the Owl Farm, passing Shoe Horn to the right.

See Ya' at the Yard, Meat (V5) A super-classic sloper line. Sit-start on a knobby left hand and two pockets for the right, make a long move with the left hand to a bad sloper gaston, and then bust up to the right sloper and the top.

See Ya' at the Yard, Meat

See Ya' at the Yard, Meat
(aka The Font Problem)

Shoe Horn (V1) A great little warm-up (make sure you stretch your back before hopping on). Sit-start on the left side of the scoop and climb the awesome features up and over to the right with some tricky body positioning. Make a move to the jug on the lip and then over the top on slopers.

Shoe Horn

Red Heat (V1) These next two routes should be taken seriously—they are very tall highballs, and you should be confident climbing at these grades. This line starts on the far right side of the wall on some good edges and moves up on pockets to a slanting seam. From here make the committing moves to the top with a scary mantle.

Peak Communism (V0) Just to the left of Red Heat is another highball gem that will keep your attention the whole way. Start on some fun pockets down low and work your way to the top on tricky slopers.

Red Heat and Peak Communism

RAT BOULDER

The Rat Boulder has become popular more recently as it has cleaned up much more than when it was discovered. A nice long traverse of the whole boulder exists here as well as the two classics listed in this guide.

Finding the boulder: As you hike down the trail toward the main boulder field, before you arrive at the base of the Ant Boulder, look for a trail that leads off to the left. Follow this trail directly to the Rat Boulder.

The Rats of Nimh (V5) Start low on the huge shelf and make a big move up to a pair of sloping edges, then another move up right to a sloping ledge, and then work your way to the top.

Chummin' (V2) Start on the right side of the huge sloping shelf and make a couple moves right to the hanging bulge and a huge hueco on its face. Move up from here and exit direct via a scary highball topout, or escape to the left by stemming over to the top of The Rats of Nimh.

Garrett Gregor sticks the crux on Grotesque Old Woman (V8) on his way to finishing off his rampage at the Brickyard for the bouldering flick *SoulCal: A Cali Bouldering Video*.

Rat Boulder

The Rats
of Nimh

Chummin'

Ant Boulder

ANT BOULDER

This is the first main boulder you run into as you follow the trail down to the boulder field; it was most likely one of the first boulders seen and climbed on in the area. The tall main face has the best routes. To descend the boulder, scramble down the tree on the right side of the boulder.

Finding the boulder: From the parking area the main trail leads directly to the base of the Ant Boulder.

Army Ant (V0) Start at the large hueco in the center of the wall and climb up the left-facing rail. You will be treated to fun moves on edges and slopers, and a topout that keeps you in the zone.

Chocolate Covered Ant (V0) An engaging climb just to the right of Army Ant. Start on the left side of the giant hueco and work your way up through edges and knobs near the top.

Piss Ant (V0) Start on the far right side of the giant hueco and climb to a big left-facing corner. Use the corner and a good edge around the right to get to the slopers on top, keep it together with good footwork, and top out.

YETI BOULDER

This is the boulder everyone comes to see, as it holds one of the finest problems in Santa Barbara, Yeti (V4). Steve Edwards, Jason Huston, and their crew discovered this boulder in the mid-1990s. The area fell into the shadows a couple times, but has now become one of the gems people travel here for.

Finding the boulder: From the parking area, follow the main trail down to the boulder field. Before you arrive at the Ant Boulder, the trail splits; take the right fork and weave through the bushes to the base of the Yeti Boulder on your right.

Sasquatch (V5) Start on the right side of the wall and use a good left-hand edge at head height and a lower

Yeti Boulder

Yeti

Sasquatch

right-hand crimp. Make a big move to the sloped dish and bump into the sidepull with the left hand. Navigate your way through slopers to the top up and right.

Yeti (V4) A mega classic for the area, a must-do. Just a few inches to the left of Sasquatch, start with your hands on a pair of good edges at head height. Move to the hueco and bump up through a series of sloping holds up and left, then continue to the top on more slopers.

CHARLOTTE'S WEB AREA

Another classic boulder was discovered in the mid-1990s and was instantly a classic with its two distinct lines—Charlotte's Web (V3)

and Grotesque Old Woman (V7/8). The surrounding blocks offer fun moderates to keep everyone in your crew happy.

Finding the boulders: From the parking area, follow the directions to the Yeti Boulder. Just past this boulder the trail splits; directly in front of you is Way Under, and to the left is the Charlotte's Web Boulder and Deep Forest Arête.

Way Under (V2) Start on awesome sculpted jugs down low and make a few moves up and to the left on more jugs, then commit and make a long move up to the sloping rail above. Continue up right on more slopers to top out.

Mary Patterson climbing the classic line, Yeti (V4)
PHOTO HJÖRDIS RICKERT-ZEUGSWETTER

Way Under

Deep Forest Arête

Deep Forest Arête

Charlotte's Web and Grotesque Old Woman

Deep Forest Arête (V0) A fun little warm-up for the area. Start low on the left arête on a large undercling and move through cool pinches, edges, and gastons to the top.

Charlotte's Web (V3) Mega classic for the grade. Start on a good edge for the right hand and a fun little sidepull pinch for the left. Work your way to the sloping ledge and easier topout above. Many variations exist.

Grotesque Old Woman (V8/10) To the right of Charlotte's Web is a stout V7 with an even harder sit start if you are up for the challenge. Begin standing with a sloping pocket sidepull and a small crimp for the right hand, then make a huge move to the sloping edge above with the right hand and a good sidepull crimp for the left. Continue up delicate sloping and compression moves to the top.

The Cave Boulder

THE CAVE BOULDER

This is a popular boulder to set up at for a few hours; the location is typically a lot cooler because of the cave and has lots of shade from the large trees. The variety of problems here spans the moderate to hard grade range and can keep a whole crew happy and working beta out for the afternoon.

Finding the boulder: Follow the directions to the Yeti Boulder; just past this boulder the trail splits; follow the trail to the right, up a short incline and to the lip of the cave where Watch the Dog begins.

Watch the Dog (V5) On the far left side of the cave, start on the huge flat blocks and make your way across the right-facing corner on sloping loafs and pinches. Lots of heel hooks will get you through to the final drop-off ledge at the lip.

Soot Patrol (V7) Start on the right side of the main cave under the honeycombs. Begin with your hands on good jugs at the base of the prow and make a big throw to a large, flat edge and then into some of the honeycomb pockets. Make a shoulder-wrenching move and follow the seam to the lip, then drop off for the V3 variation or continue on tricky slopers over the lip of the cave.

The Cave Boulder

Soot Patrol

The Cave Boulder

Mister Witty (V7) Around the corner from Soot Patrol is a giant hueco at ground level; start sitting in here and work your way to some sloping edges at the lip of the roof. Bump up to another patina edge where you can match and figure out how to squirm your feet over the lip while negotiating bad slopers.

All Mod Cons (V9) Start left hand in a hueco undercling and right hand on the corner feature. Make a large move over the lip with the right hand to a decent edge you can match; from here move up on tricky pinches and slopers using a heel hook to get the large sloping edge up high with the right hand. Continue straight up the tall and delicate slab.

All Mods On (V6) The easier variation to All Mod Cons. Start the same, but instead of going directly up the slab, move a little out right and use the larger holds around the corner.

Points of Interest and History
In May 2009 the Jesusita fire ripped across the area, revealing more boulders. Once again development began at the Brickyard, with new offshoot areas not described in this book being developed by smaller crews, showing that this area still has potential for the right eyes and hands!

In 2006 the Brickyard was one of the featured climbing areas in producer Paul Dusatko's epic bouldering film *SoulCal: A Cali Bouldering Video,* where the likes of Natasha Barnes and Garrett Gregor threw down on the boulders in the forest here.

The Cave Boulder

Standing on the Corner Watching All the Girls Go By

Standing on the Corner Watching All the Girls Go By (V4) Start down in the same corner as the previous two routes, but this time move out of the cave to the right through some large holds, then head straight up to a seam and up the scary slab.

DANCING OUTLAW BOULDER

This area was really put on the map when Bob Banks put up the mega classic The Dancing Outlaw (V8). This boulder has seen the most recent development in the area with amazing new link-ups and independent lines.

Finding the boulder: Follow the directions to the Cave Boulder; the boulder opposite the main overhang of the cave is the backside of the Dancing Outlaw Boulder.

Garrett Gregor grabs one more loaf on his way to the top of Smooth Criminal (V7), a route with some of the best slopers on the hill.

Old and in the Way (V3) This climb is hiding behind a tree just at your back from the Cave Boulder. Start on a good edge and a pocket, then make some moves up a good right-facing flake and a sloper rail for the left hand.

Dancing Outlaw Boulder

Old and in the Way

Smooth Criminal (V7) Another super classic for the grade. Start sitting with your hands on opposing sidepulls and make a move with your left hand to an edge at the lip. From here reach up high to a sloper out right and balance your way to the top.

Lonesome Pine (V5) This is the stand start to Smooth Criminal. Begin on the sloping arête and a good edge, then make the final balancy moves up the face.

Dancing Outlaw Boulder

Smooth Criminal

Dancing Outlaw Boulder

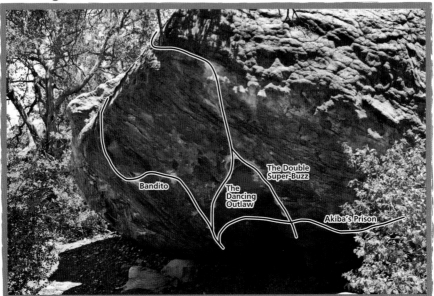

The Dancing Outlaw (V8) A must-do if this is in your grade range. Start sitting on the left side of the human-sized hueco and climb up the rib, eventually getting a good left-hand edge outside the hueco. Reposition and get the top of the hueco as an undercling, then make the huge move up over the lip to the giant sloper. Match on the sloper and traverse out left to exit.

The Double Super-Buzz (V8) Start on the right side of the large hueco and climb up to join the top of The Dancing Outlaw.

Akiba's Prison (V8) This is a nice, long endurance traverse that takes you through some great movement. Begin at The Dancing Outlaw and traverse right, through the hueco and out the right side to a series of under-clings that will lead you to the start of Smooth Criminal. Finish up through the slopers on that route.

Bandito (V9) Start as for The Dancing Outlaw, but once you hit the good edge outside the hueco, continue to move left along the rail out to the sloping corner where you make a series of bumps with your left hand. Make the final bump to the sloper on the lip and mantle.

12.

Lizard's Mouth

Lizard's Mouth is the most extensive bouldering area in Santa Barbara County. This book only includes the best of the best, but a climber could spend multiple years coming back to this area and constantly discovering something new. With 300-plus documented climbs established over the years, "The Mouth" is a maze of wind-sculpted sandstone boulders and slabs that all lead to the namesake Itself, the Lizard's Mouth, a huge overhang resembling a lizard that looks out over the Pacific Ocean and the town of Santa Barbara. The view from the top of the Lizard's Mouth alone is worth the visit; from here you have a 360-degree view of the surrounding area and down the Pacific coastline toward Ventura, out to the Channel Islands, and toward the Santa Ynez and San Rafael Mountain ranges. This is definitely the spot to see the morning mists roll over to the warmer Santa Ynez Valley or to catch a killer sunset.

The Chumash Indian tribes cherished this landscape when they lived here over the course of their 13,000 years on this land. The mountains above Santa Barbara were of special importance, being the center of their territory and cultural circle. It's easy to imagine a lone Chumash tribesman standing tall atop the Lizard's Mouth watching the ocean, clouds, and land pass beneath his feet.

Climbing at the Mouth is rumored to have begun in the 1970s, with most of the climbing done on toprope around the Lizard's Mouth cave. In 1992 someone unfortunately put bolt anchors in the top of the Mouth—where you can clearly build your own anchor—but it is quite likely that this helped spur more interest from climbers in the area. In 1996 the strongly motivated crew from "The Castle" sieged the Mouth over the course of one summer. The large crew led by Steve Edwards, John Perlin, Todd Mei, Wills Young, and Arvind Gupta added over 200 quality boulder problems, clearly putting Lizard's Mouth on the map once and for all. When Bob Banks came out with his guidebook Oceans 11 in 2003, another 100 problems had been added, mainly with the help of Kelly Lindsay, Forest Weaver, Bob Banks, and their motivated crew. The development continues to this day with Bernd Zeugswetter's latest addition, Egret Arête (V10 R), in 2008.

Lizard's Mouth is a popular hiking destination for locals and visitors

Lizard's Mouth

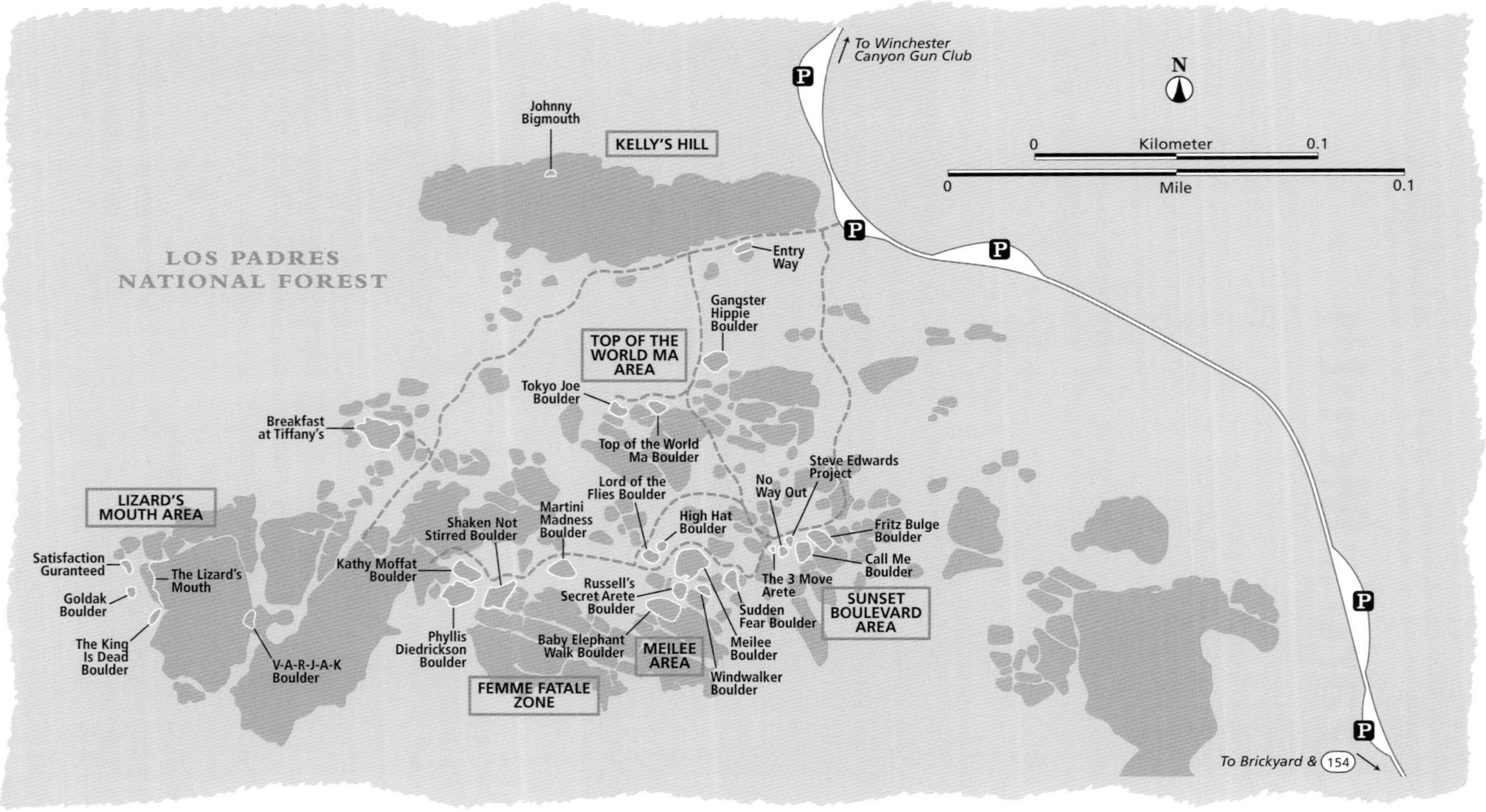

LOS PADRES NATIONAL FOREST

KELLY'S HILL

Johnny Bigmouth

Entry Way

Gangster Hippie Boulder

TOP OF THE WORLD MA AREA

Top of the World Ma Boulder

Tokyo Joe Boulder

Lord of the Flies Boulder

Martini Madness Boulder

Russell's Secret Arete Boulder

Steve Edwards Project

No Way Out

High Hat Boulder

The 3 Move Arete

Sudden Fear Boulder

Meilee Boulder

Windwalker Boulder

MEILEE AREA

Fritz Bulge Boulder

Call Me Boulder

SUNSET BOULEVARD AREA

Baby Elephant Walk Boulder

FEMME FATALE ZONE

Shaken Not Stirred Boulder

Phyllis Diedrickson Boulder

Kathy Moffat Boulder

Breakfast at Tiffany's

V-A-R-J-A-K Boulder

The Lizard's Mouth

Satisfaction Guranteed

Goldak Boulder

The King Is Dead Boulder

LIZARD'S MOUTH AREA

To Winchester Canyon Gun Club

To Brickyard & 154

N

Kilometer

Mile

0   0.1

0   0.1   0.1

alike, so please be courteous and pack out all your trash and pick up any other trash you see. There is an annual volunteer cleanup here, and it is standard fare to see 90-plus pounds of trash collected; please do your part to keep it clean.

Getting there: From US 101 North or South, take exit 101b for State Street and CA 154/Cachuma Lake. At the end of the ramp, drive north on CA 154 for 7.1 miles into the mountains to the junction with West Camino Cielo Road on your left. Turn here and follow this winding road for 3.7 miles to pullouts on your right and left. At the end of the road is the Winchester Canyon Gun Club.

Finding the boulders: From the pullouts, walk to the ocean side of the road and locate a hiker's trailhead with a trashcan on the left. The main trail and other spur trails lead to all the climbing areas.

In a bouldering paradise, a lone climber gets his last lap on Lord of the Flies (V0+).
PHOTO SEAN NAUGLE

ENTRY WAY

This is the first boulder seen when hiking in on the main trail, so it's easy to see why there are a few easy warm-ups on this block. This guide only lists the best line, but there are a handful of fun options at this first stop.

Finding the boulder: From the road, follow the main trail for a couple hundred feet to the boulder on the left side of the trail.

Entry Way

Crossfire

Kelly's Hill

Johnny
Bigmouth

Crossfire (V2) It's inevitable if this is your first time here: You will drop your pads at this first boulder and climb something. There are a bunch of good V0s on the boulder, but the standouts are on the arête. For this V2, climb the arête without using the hold on the huge rib around the left corner. Johnny Rocco is a V0 variation that uses the holds on the rib.

KELLY'S HILL

The first set of slabs on your right that you encounter from the entrance to Lizard's Mouth hosts only a handful of boulders large enough to climb on, but the route listed in this guide is worth the short hike.

Finding the boulder: Follow the trail just past the Entry Way Boulder and start up the slabs on the right. Continue up at an angle away from the road; you will notice some larger boulders near the top of the slabs. You should be able to walk there with little or no rock scrambling. Johnny Bigmouth faces away from the road.

Johnny Bigmouth (V4) Start sitting in the large hueco on the right side. Climb the rib and make a long move out right to a decent edge, then go for the sloper on the lip with the left hand. Finish up a few more slopers and end with a mantle.

BREAKFAST AT TIFFANY'S

This small cluster of boulders is hidden from view, but is quite a great spot to warm up not only your fingers but also your mind with the epic wide crack, Touch of Evil. It may take some effort to find these boulders, but once you do I guarantee everyone in your crew will find a line that they just love and need to repeat. The exterior of the entrance to the boulders contains some good tall moderates not listed in this guide.

Finding the boulder: Follow the main trail past the Entry Way Boulder for a couple more minutes, passing a few more large boulders as you weave your way slightly to the left. Just before you approach the next big set of slabs where the Lizard's Mouth can be found, there is a cluster of boulders at the end of the slabs. To the right a small climber's trail leads to a tall boulder with a large cave underneath; it is easiest to scramble under the boulder to access the Breakfast at Tiffany's climbing area.

Charade (V2) Start on the short slab to the right of the corner. Climb up to the ledge and use a pocket on the face to climb straight to the top.

Funny Face (V0) Start the same as Charade, but when you get your hands on the ledge, move to the right and follow the line of pockets and jugs to the top.

Breakfast at Tiffany's

My Fair Lady (V1 R) Scramble around the corner from the previous routes to find this little gem. Climb up big holds and make a big move to a large ledge in the middle of the wall. From the ledge continue through pockets over the lip of the overhang. The landing is bad, so make sure to have pads and spotters.

Breakfast at Tiffany's

Touch of Evil

Touch of Evil (V0 R) Follow the main wall down to the right until you come upon this monster crack. The crux is getting into the wide crack, then easy climbing on fun holds leads the way to the top of this highball.

TOP OF THE WORLD MA

This area has seen some of the more recent development with the addition of the classic Gangster Hippie (V6/7). It's easy to pass over when hiking to the Sunset Boulevard and Meilee areas because the boulders sit on the cusp of a small cliff band on the hill. This is a good location to escape any crowds that are commonly found in the more popular areas. Many boulder problems exist among the maze of boulders here, in particular a lot of V0 to V2s.

Finding the boulders: From the road follow the main trail 100 feet past the Entry Way Boulder to a small climber's trail leading off to the left toward a short hill with a cliff band. You can see the Gangster Hippie Boulder facing you on the hillside. Hike up the trail to the boulders.

Gangster Hippie (V6/7) Start on the large, curving rail and make some tough moves to slopers out left on the face and the corner; from here climb straight up through more slopers to the top.

Top of the World Ma

Gangster Hippie

Suburban Hippie (V0) On the back-side of the boulder, climb up the left side of the face on a variety of large holds to the top. Another fun V0 exists on the right side of the face up the seam.

Top of the World Ma

Suburban Hippie

Top of the World Ma (V2) Start on a ledge on the blunt arête and use small holds to establish onto the boulder, then work your way up through slopers to the top.

Top of the World Ma

Top of the World Ma

Little Bear (V7) Around the corner to the left of Top of the World Ma. Start on a jug rail under the prow, make a big move up to the arête, and use bad sloping edges to climb your way to the top.

Key Largo (V2) Start standing on the left of the arête; use good underclings and jugs to climb straight up.

Top of the World Ma

Little Bear

Koala Bear (V6) This is the sit start to Key Largo. Start on a large undercling under the roof and use slopers on the face to power out to the starting holds of Key Largo out left. Finish up the arête.

Tokyo Joe (V3) Just to the right of the arête, use a trio of sidepulls to work your way up to better holds on top.

Top of the World Ma

Tokyo Joe

Key Largo/
Koala Bear

SUNSET BOULEVARD

A fantastic area to set up base camp for a half day, there is enough here to keep everyone climbing, projecting, and certainly getting scared on the classic highballs. Sunset Boulevard showcases some amazing wind-sculpted huecos and caves that you can actually climb on—be sure to check out the awesome slopers on A Steve Edwards Project (V4) and Call Me (V6). If you are an aficionado of highballs, then this is definitely the sector for you, with such greats as Experiment in Terror (V2) and Serious as a Deacon (V1 R), the latter definitely not for the faint of heart even though it showcases the easier grade.

Finding the boulders: From the road enter the main trail and take the small climber's trail immediately to the left just past the trashcan. Follow this trail up a short hill through a small cluster of rocks and through a clearing to the large boulders ahead and to the right—this is Sunset Boulevard.

Fritz Bulge (V6) A must-do for anyone who can climb in this range and likes a good highball. Start low in the beautiful sculpted holds in the hueco, climb out the left side, and make a long move to the sloping hueco on the face. Match this up and power up to two sloping edges and a final committing move to a bad sloper.

Experiment in Terror (V2) Just to the right of Fritz Bulge. Start using the sculpted holds in the huceo for your left hand, make moves up toward two decent holds on a small ledge, and continue up for a committing topout.

On the long sought after first ascent of Egret Arête (V10 R), Bernd Zeugswetter makes no mistakes on his way to the summit of this beauty. Photo Sean Naugle

Sunset Boulevard

Panic in the Streets (V3) On the right side of the boulder, look for two good crimps on the face; use these to make a long move up and left to another edge, then high step and use slopers on your way to the top.

Sunset Boulevard

Call Me (V6) This line has a hold that has seen some work done to it; purists like to skip the left-handed edge and bust straight to the sloper on top from the hueco for full value. The climb is still fun using the left-hand edge and goes at V4.

Take Five (V5) Just around the corner to the left of Call Me. Start on two bad slopers and try to get established and make a move to the sloping lip of a hueco; continue desperately to top out on slopers.

Sunset Boulevard

Serious as a Deacon (V1 R) A very serious endeavor indeed. Start with your hands in the base of a large hueco, then climb through the hueco and make a long reach to a bad sloper; continue the nerve-racking journey on slopers to the top.

Sunset Boulevard

Serious as a Deacon

Double Indemnity (V1 R) A good tall warm-up for the area. Start below a giant hueco and climb to and past it toward worse holds.

Sunset Boulevard (V0) Just to the right of Double Indemnity, this fun warm-up climbs up a low-angle wall to a small hueco; continue on good terrain to the top.

Sunset Boulevard

No Way Out (V0 R) Begin with both hands in a big hueco, then climb up and right through a good edge to a sloping rail at the top and a highball finish.

Sunset Boulevard

A Steve Edwards Project (V4) Steve did not get the first ascent of this little gem, as Mike Collee climbed it first in the late 1990s. Use a series of slopers and sidepulls and a possible heel hook to work your way to the top.

Sunset Boulevard

A Steve Edwards Project

The 3 Move Arête (V5) On your way to the Sudden Fear Boulder and Meilee area, you will walk by this short arête on your left. Sit-start and use a variety of ways to climb through the arête to a jug on top. Good fun.

Sunset Boulevard

The 3-Move Arête

MEILEE AREA

This is definitely the spot to hang out if you aren't at the Lizard's Mouth cave. The Meilee cave may be one-tenth the height of the Lizard's Mouth, but it has so many entertaining lines and myriad exits that it surely will have you coming back for more tricep-pumping action. There are a slew of hidden problems around the main cave that should not be missed, like the stunning crack plucked from another world, Moon River (5.7), or the New Age sloper battle, Windwalker (V7). Also be sure to check out High Hat (V5) and Lord of the Flies (V0+), two classics out in the open.

Finding the boulders: Follow the directions to Sunset Boulevard and continue across the small gully from The 3 Move Arête; you can see the main face of the Sudden Fear Boulder from here. Meilee is just around the right corner of this boulder.

Dressed to impress, Steve Edwards hucks a lap on Take Five (V5) during the heyday of Santa Barbara development. PHOTO JASON HOUSTON

Meilee Area

She Had Nothing to Do with It

(V6) Start sitting on the far left arête on a good hold and an undercling. Climb up the arête for a move or use the hole out right to get to a jug and some good edges on the face to the right of the arête. From here make a big move to gain a slanting edge around the left corner and finish up the left side of the arête.

Sudden Fear

(V1) Start just right of the arête on a large hole and move up through a large hueco toward less than positive holds on top—an exciting highball finish.

Desperate Hours

(V3) Start on the Sudden Fear jug and stay low to traverse right, then make a long throw right to a deep slot to join Nightmare Alley. Continue to the top from here.

Nightmare Alley

(V1) Start on the deep slot on the right side of the wall and move up through some jugs and good edges to a slightly less spooky topout than on the left side of the boulder.

Meilee Area

Faided, Fat, Greedy Women (V4)
Start on the far left side of the cave at the base of a blunt prow and climb through good edges, slopers, and underclings to an awesome direct mantle exit.

Ace in the Hole (V2) Just to the right of Faided, Fat, Greedy Women. Start at the bottom of a thin crack and follow it to the lip for some sweet finger-locking action over the lip.

Meilee (V3/4) Start in the heart of the cave and use a multitude of jug holds under the roof and the sloping lip on the outside of the roof to traverse right

for the length of the cave until you reach a natural mantle point. A great way to get the juices flowing in the morning, the traverse can be reversed as well at about the same grade.

13 Men (V2) On the right side of the cave there is a wide crack in the roof; start here and use great holds to exit left out of the cave to the lip, then traverse right a little to the mantle of Meilee.

Knock on Any Door (V1) Start the same as 13 Men and climb out of the roof through big jugs to the right, then mantle as for Meilee.

Moon River (5.7) From the Meilee boulder, walk around the left corner to discover a hidden cove of gems. The first problem you will encounter is the stunning hands to wide crack, Moon River.

Meilee Area

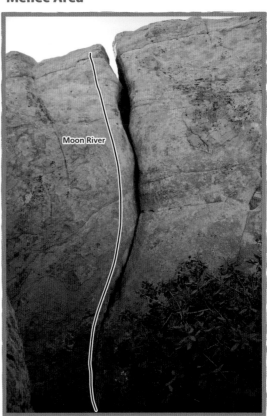

Moon River

In the zone, Geneva Damico sets her sights on the next big throw under the Meilee roof.

PHOTO SEAN NAUGLE

Breathless (V3) Continue to follow the wall around to the right to find this stunning blunt arête. Start on the low boulder and get some decent sidepulls for the left hand and dishes on the right face; work your way up this way before you commit to the face and topout. Brings pads and a spotter for this tall boy.

Meilee Area

Breathless

Windwalker (V7) Start low on decent edges and work your way onto the arête with your right hand and the water runnel with your left hand. Finish up to the top on easier terrain.

The Commitment (V6) Just behind Breathless and the Windwalker Boulder is a concentrated little area. Begin The Commitment at a hueco in the middle of the wall; use good holds and a tiny crimp to start and bad slopers on top.

Meilee Area

Windwalker

Russell's Secret Arête (V6) Compress your way up this blank arête to a terrifying topout on slopers. Be sure to bring lots of pads and spotters.

Bedroom Dic (V0) A great warm-up wall just opposite of the previous two climbs. Follow a line of depressions up the right side of the slabby wall.

Baby Elephant Walk (V0) Begin on the far left side of the wall and ascend a bulging slab to exciting slopers on the topout. This little gem has a great view on top.

Meilee Area

Lord of the Flies (V0+) From the Meilee Boulder continue west along the trail; Lord of the Flies is the tall pinnacle on your right as you enter a small clearing. Start on good edges and move up to a jug, then lieback a blunt flake to make a big move out left to a ledge. Get your feet up on the ledge and to better holds on top—a wonderful highball.

Meilee Area

Lord of the Flies

High Hat (V5) Just around the corner from Lord of the Flies is this shorty but goodie. Begin at the base of the blunt arête with a bad foot, a sloping left hand, and a good right hand in a slot. Make a big move with the right into the bottom of the big seam and compress your way to the top.

Meilee Area

Femme Fatale Zone

FEMME FATALE ZONE

This small sector contains some real gems along with problems ranging from V0 to V10—a little something for everyone. Most recently this area has seen development with the addition of Egret Arête (V10 R). The Martini Madness Boulder surely sees some of the most action with its outstanding warm-ups and finger-destroying hard line, Shaken, Like a Tornado (V6).

Finding the boulders: Follow the directions to the Meilee area. From the Lord of the Flies Boulder, continue walking west on the trail for a couple hundred feet to the Martini Madness Boulder, which is the start of the Femme Fatale Zone.

Martini Madness (V0) A great warm-up. Begin on the left side of the huge hueco or at the base of the left arête. Move up the arête to the highest point and mantle over.

Swingin' Singles (V2) On the far right side of the wall, start on the left side of the large hueco and climb straight up through small edges, which seem to keep getting smaller.

Shaken, Like a Tornado (V6) Begin on the right side of the sculpted hueco and make desperate and long moves on sharp holds up the blunt arête to a hard mantle.

Femme Fatale Zone

Swingin'
Singles

Shaken, Like
a Tornado

Shaken, Not Stirred (V3) Just beyond the Martini Madness boulder is this gem. Start low on slopers and compress up the bulge to a big dish on the face, then use another hueco and an edge to climb into the final mantle.

Egret Arête (V10 R) One of the newer additions to the area. Bernd Zeugswetter was the first to step up and climb this stunning arête without a rope; it has yet to see a second ascent. Start at the base on the left side of the arête with a pinch for the right hand and an edge for the left. Work your way up the arête and eventually over to the right side via some balancy and airy moves. Thrilling!

Femme Fatale Zone

Shaken, Not Stirred

Femme Fatale Zone

Egret Arête

Phyllis Diedrickson (V2) Start on the sloping ledge and work your way up the arête, then make a big move right to a good sloper and finish up with a mantle over the top. It is possible to start lower in the cave and make this a good V5.

Femme Fatale Zone

Phyllis Diedrickson

Brigid O'Shaunessy (V0) A fun
warm-up. Climb up the left side of the
low-angle wall on good edges.

Femme Fatale Zone

Femme Fatale Zone

Irene Jensen/Gilda

Kathy Moffat

Kathy Moffat (V3 R) Sit-start on the bottom of the arête with a good pocket, then make a long move up to some good edges on the face and over the top on slopers. Don't deck!

Gilda (V1) Start standing on the far right side of the boulder at the arête and make the long traverse to the left using the sloping lip and heel hooks; mantle when appropriate.

Irene Jensen (V5) Start the same as for Kathy Moffat, but instead of going to the right up the arête, climb into Gilda and complete the long traverse.

LIZARD'S MOUTH AREA

The main cave of the Lizard's Mouth is likely the first location that was climbed here on toprope. Not to be missed are the boulders at the base of the cave holding some stellar little gems like Lost Continent (V1) and Goldak (V0). If you are into highballs or want to set up a toprope, be sure to get on the wicked fun and tall Yellow Belly (V0/5.10-). You are likely to run across a lot of day hikers and tourists at this spot, as the area is the main recreational draw for people; do your part and pick up all trash you come across to help keep this area preserved for future generations.

This section also includes one excellent boulder problem on the way to the Mouth, V-A-R-J-A-K (V1). It sits

SoCal native Natasha Barnes takes her third lap of the day on Yellow Belly (V0/5.10-) for the film *SoulCal: A Cali Bouldering Video.*

in the middle of a fun little lowball area called Sit There and Take It Like a Man—a great area to relax, soak in the views, and play around on fun lowballs scattered across the main slabs here.

Finding the boulders: To access the Lizard's Mouth from the parking area, you have two main trail options. The most direct is to take the trail past Entry Way and toward the Breakfast at Tiffany's area. The trail makes a left-hand turn past Breakfast at Tiffany's to the base of the main slabs leading back to the Mouth. Walk up the slabs toward the obvious V-A-R-J-A-K Boulder sitting between a large crack running down the slabs. From here you can continue toward the Mouth.

At The King Is Dead Boulder you will find a small trail to scramble down to the lower level; continue to the right along the path to find the main Lizard's Mouth formation. The other route is to hike up the hill on the left at the start of the trail to the Sunset Boulevard area and weave your way through the boulders past the Femme Fatale Zone to the start of the slabs leading back to the Lizard's Mouth.

V-A-R-J-A-K (V1) A great little problem to hop on while heading to the main Lizard's Mouth area. Start under the overhang on large holds and make a long reach around the lip to the sloping bottom of a hueco, then top out.

Lizard's Mouth Area

The King Is Dead (V6) Stand-start the arête, then use a variety of pockets and edges on the right face while heel hooking and using sloping edges to find the final scoops up top.

King Dinosaur (V7) Just to the right of The King Is Dead, start on two slots and make a hard deadpoint to a sharp crimp up high and just to the left of a small bulge. One easier move gets you to the top lip.

Lizard's Mouth Area

The King Is Dead

King Dinosaur

Barney (V1) As you walk toward the Lizard's Mouth, Barney will be on your right. Start sitting at a large hueco, make a couple moves to gain the ledge above, and finish up on easy terrain.

Lizard's Mouth Area

Lost Continent (V1) This freestanding block hosts two great warm-ups. This climb faces toward the Lizard's Mouth and starts in the cave. Make a move out to the shelf on the right and use fun jugs to climb up the featured face.

Lizard's Mouth Area

Lost Continent

Goldak

Lizard's Mouth Area

Goldak (V0) On the backside of the same boulder, climb the wonderful curving crack with plenty of jugs to the summit.

Lizard's Mouth Traverse (V0 and up) Make this what you want it to be; pick a spot and go—left or right, up or down—there are so many variations. The classic V0 start begins on the right side of the wall and traverses left until you can step off on the rocks at the other end.

Yellow Belly (V0/5.10-) Start standing (or sitting to add some extra climbing) and climb through a series of large holds out the roof toward a small, honeycombed section of the face. Bust up to a large shelf from here and continue the highball journey to the left-facing flake and jugs above. Basically a free solo if you plan to climb the whole line ropeless.

Lizard's Mouth Area

Satisfaction Guaranteed (V3) Down below the plateau of the Lizard's Mouth cave hides a nice little over-hanging problem. Scramble down a couple boulders to get to the start of the route. Begin sitting on pockets and an awesome undercling feature; make a big move to the shelf and then up to the top on small edges.

Points of Interest and History

The Husahkiws, or Wind Caves, are located in this region, a series of wind-carved caves and huecos found among the hillsides off the Camino Cielo, holding hidden glimpses into Chumash history. Artwork graces the walls of these Husahkiws and depicts a variety of stories. The art was made with charcoal, red ochre, and crushed shells.

Part of the Santa Barbara bouldering legend is "The Castle." According to an article from the *Santa Barbara Independent*, the climbers' hot spot in the 1990s was a house called "The Castle," which had a nearly 600-square-foot indoor/outdoor climbing structure designed for training. It not only was a place to practice the sport, but it also acted as a flophouse for climbers traveling through Santa Barbara. At certain times there might be several people staying in the house and maybe ten camped in the backyard. This was a peak period for the sport, when many climbing routes in the hills were being established.

In June 2014 the Lizard's Mouth was the scene of installation art dubbed *Yarnbomb*. Mastermind artist Stephen Duneier organized over 388 contributors from thirty-six countries to help knit wraps out of yarn for the boulders. Stephen and his team decorated the area and unveiled it to the public for just a few days, and then it disappeared to a new location.

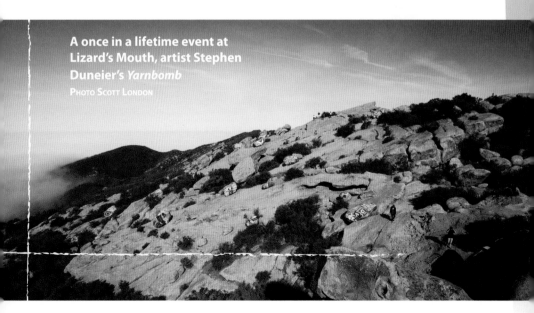

A once in a lifetime event at Lizard's Mouth, artist Stephen Duneier's *Yarnbomb*
PHOTO SCOTT LONDON

Young gun Bryson Fienup nears the top of He Who Double-Crosses Me . . . (5.8).
PHOTO MATTHEW FIENUP

13.

Crag Full O' Dynamite

If you are looking for a real easy afternoon or are taking some new climbers to the cliff for the first time, then this is the place for you. All the way on the far eastern stretches of the Camino Cielo lies this short beginner's cliff right on the side of the road. You won't see much automobile traffic on this end of the road, so it's a fairly safe place to climb considering its location. When Steve Edwards originally developed this crag, it was received with skepticism due to the proximity to the road, but as time went on, people realized it had its purpose. The crag sees a lot of shade during the day due to its northwestern-facing cliff, and the routes are well equipped, but always be aware of loose rock—the sandstone always has the potential to break.

Getting there: From US 101 North take exit 95 for Salinas Street. Follow Salinas Street for 0.9 mile to a traffic circle and take the second exit onto Sycamore Canyon Road (CA

Crag Full O' Dynamite

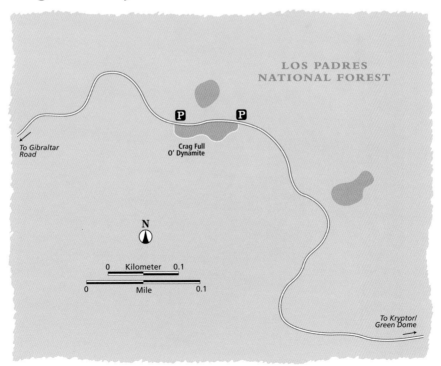

144). Follow this for 1.1 miles and keep left at the bend onto Stanwood Drive (CA 192). Continue for another 1.1 miles and take a right onto Cielito Road. Follow this for 0.5 mile and turn right onto Gibraltar Road (FR 5N40). Continue on this windy road for 6.2 miles until you see East Camino Cielo on your right. Follow this beautiful ridgeline road for 5.1 miles. You can see the cliff on your right, and there are a couple of pullouts on the left (north) side of the road as you approach the crag.

Finding the crag: Access is from the parking at the base of the crag.

Once Upon a Climb in the West (5.9) On the far left end of the crag, start just to the left of a left-facing corner system and climb up through a tricky start toward the final crux mantle to the anchors. 4 bolts to a 2-bolt anchor.

For a Few Crystals More (5.9) This route starts to the right of the left-facing corner system. Climb up easy terrain to clip a high first bolt, then

Crag Full O'Dynamite

continue up the wall to a high slab crux after the third bolt. Clip one more bolt on the way to the anchors. 4 bolts to 2 bolt anchors.

Fistful of Crystals (5.8 TR) Due to the occasional loose rock on this route, this is a toprope that is the direct line to The Good, the Bad, and the Ugly. Start directly under the trees near the anchors, then climb up toward the large roof and surmount it to the anchors.

The Good, the Bad, and the Ugly
(5.9) The best line at the crag. Start on the slab and climb up and left, clipping five bolts on the way. After the fifth bolt climb straight up toward the roof. Make a funky crux move to clip the seventh bolt over the roof; this move can be protected with an extra 0.5-inch piece of gear. Continue on easier terrain to the anchors. 8 bolts to 2 bolt anchors.

Arch Stanton (5.6 TR) The next three routes all share the same anchors.

Climb The Ecstasy of Gold to toprope this line and the next. Follow the right-facing corner that arches up the face, then traverse right to the anchors. Beware of loose rock.

Unknown (5.7 TR) The direct line for the anchors. Start on a small apron of rock and climb up through some unique formations on the way to the anchors.

The Ecstasy of Gold (5.8) For such a short route, this is some of the best rock on the wall; it was bolted by Steve Edwards in 1992. Follow the line of great crimps up the face. 4 bolts to a 2-bolt anchor.

My Name's Nobody, Bub (5.8) If someone in your group is learning to climb, this may be the best short route to help keep his or her nerves down. A mere two bolts to a single cold shut make this a nice testing ground for newbies.

Steve Edwards and his crew had some fun with the names at this crag. If you are a Clint Eastwood fan, then everything here should make your smile a little bigger when climbing. The classic line from Clint's character Blondie, "It was the grave marked 'unknown' right beside Arch Stanton" was from the film *The Good, the Bad and the Ugly* and is a clue as to where some of the names came from.

He Who Double-Crosses Me and Leaves Me Alone, He Understands Nothing about Tuco ... Nothing (5.8) On the far right side of the crag is a nice route that begins on a short slab to the right of a left-facing corner. Climb up to a small roof and continue up the easier slab to the anchors. 4 bolts to a 2-bolt anchor.

Don't tag Ojai!
Beautify our home!

Appendix

Gear Shops

Great Pacific Iron Works: Patagonia
235 West Santa Clara St.
Ventura, CA 93001
(805) 643-6074

Mountain Air Sports
14 State St.
Santa Barbara, CA 93101
(805) 962-0049

Real Cheap Sports
36 West Santa Clara St.
Ventura, CA 93001
(805) 648-3803

REI
2700 Seaglass Way
Oxnard, CA 93036
(805) 981-1938

REI
321 Anacapa St.
Santa Barbara, CA 93101
(805) 560-1938

Gyms

Boulderdash
880 Hampshire Rd., Ste. A
Thousand Oaks, CA 91361
(805) 557-1300

Crux Climbing Center
1160 Laurel Ln.
San Luis Obispo, CA 93401
(805) 544-2789

Goleta Valley Athletic Club
170 Los Carneros Way
Goleta, CA 93117
(805) 968-1023

Santa Barbara Rock Gym
322 State St.
Santa Barbara, CA 93101
(805) 770-3225

SLO-Op Climbing
289 Prado Rd.
San Luis Obispo, CA 93401
(805) 720-1245

Vertical Heaven
5600 Everglades St.
Ventura, CA 93003
(805) 339-9022

Guide Services (Southern California Area)

ATS Adventureworks, (626) 434-3636

Earthworks, (805) 320-2739

On Rope Consulting, (310) 804-7303

Sierra Mountaineering International, (760) 872-4929

Sierra Rock Climbing School, (760) 937-6762

Southern California Mountaineers Association, www.rockclimbing.org

Vertical Adventures, (800) 514-8785

Wilderness Outings, (877) 494-5368

Hospitals

Community Memorial Hospital
147 North Brent St.
Ventura, CA 93003
(805) 652-5011

Goleta Valley Cottage Hospital
351 South Patterson Ave.
Santa Barbara, CA 93111
(805) 681-6473

MedCenter Inc.
319 North Milpas St.
Santa Barbara, CA 93103
(805) 965-3011

Santa Barbara Cottage Hospital
400 West Pueblo St.
Santa Barbara, CA 93105
(805) 682-7111

St. John's Regional Medical Center
1600 North Rose Ave.
Oxnard, CA 93030
(805) 988-2500

Ventura County Medical Center
3291 Loma Vista Rd.
Ventura, CA 93003
(805) 652-6000

Ventura Urgent Care Center
5725 Ralston St., #101
Ventura, CA 93003
(805) 658-2273

West Ventura Urgent Care
133 West Santa Clara St.
Ventura, CA 93001
(805) 641-5620

Index

About the Author

Damon Corso, a freelance photographer, writer, and videographer, has been photographing and filming rock climbing professionals for the past twelve years across the United States and Europe. His work can be found on the covers and in feature articles of a multitude of major magazines, such as *Climbing*, *Rock & Ice*, *Deadpoint*, *Urban Climber*, *Los Angeles Magazine*, *Time Magazine*, *National Geographic Adventure*, and *Exercise & Health Magazine*. His work is also on display at the Museum of Photography in Bad Ischl, Austria. Damon and his wife, Crystalyn, currently live in Southern California, where he dreams of spending a majority of his time searching the High Sierra for untouched granite boulders.

PROTECTING CLIMBING ACCESS SINCE 1991

JOIN US
WWW.ACCESSFUND.ORG

Jonathan Siegrist, Third Millenium (14a), the Monastery, CO. Photo by: Keith Ladzinski